COMMUNICATION
AMONG SOCIAL BEES

WITHDRAW

Martin Lindauer
Zoological Institute,
University of Munich

HARVARD UNIVERSITY PRESS
CAMBRIDGE, MASSACHUSETTS ~ 1961

PREFACE

WHEN I WAS INVITED by Harvard University to deliver the Prather Lectures in Biology, in the spring of 1959, I was at first hesitant to accept this honor. By our German standards, I was much too young to undertake such lectures especially at one of the most famous universities, in a series to which many illustrious workers had previously contributed.

I was then all the more surprised and pleased that these lectures met with such great interest—not only from experts in the field, and not only within Harvard, but also in eight other North American universities where I received additional invitations to deliver one or two of these lectures.

I am deeply grateful for this opportunity to tell something about our recent work on bees, which is essentially a continuation of the work reported on at Harvard by Professor von Frisch in 1949. And I should like to express my thanks for the generous hospitality with which I was everywhere received. This interest and this kind hospitality gave me hope and inspiration for further work; for from it I now recognized that common problems and interests within biology have built new bridges, bridges that span wrongs of the past and transcend all national boundaries, making possible again friendships between all countries.

I should like to dedicate this little book to my revered teacher, Professor von Frisch, who introduced me to the wonderland of the bees' society.

M. L.

Munich
May, 1960

CONTENTS

~

FIGURES

CONTENTS

CONTENTS

COMMUNICATION
AMONG SOCIAL BEES

1

Elementary Forms
of Communication

~ Introduction ~

IN THE LAST ANALYSIS, all animals are social beings. They are all obliged to form at least temporary alliances, in order to ensure the continuity of their species. In the simplest case, the sexual partners meet each other for mating. And when the partnership extends beyond mating until the time when the offspring appear, we are already dealing with a social unit, the family. This "family community" reaches its highest development in the social insects.

Of a different kind are the "interest communities," which consist of members of the same species from a certain area, joined for mutual protection, as a feeding community, or as a mating community.

In every case a prerequisite of such alliances and social communities is the ability to communicate with each other. The members must be able to inform each other at least that they belong to the same species; furthermore, they have to give information as to what position they occupy in the social hierarchy, as to when they are ready for mating, and what mood they are in at that moment. They may even give instructions for duties that must be performed for the sake of the community life.

There are chemical, optical, and mechanical means of communication at the disposal of the animals. The most primitive communication undoubtedly takes place by *chemical* means: the Protozoa attract one another chemically. The information that they mediate is rather meager, but it is sufficient and unequivocal: membership in a certain species and readiness for copulation are announced in this way.

The many kinds of sexual attractants in higher animals, which serve to bring male and female together, also have a chemical basis; either the female or the male may be the attracting partner. This method of communication must be considered primitive too, since practically no means of variation are inherent in the scent language, in contrast to the optical or acoustical signals. To differentiate scent signals, different scents must be emitted from different scent glands. The stag, for instance, can broadcast two kinds of scent signals: one to mark the trail and keep the herd together, and the other to inform rivals of the boundaries of his territory. But for these two kinds of information he needs two anatomically separated glands: the hoof glands and the eye glands.

In contrast to scent signals, optical signals are richly varied. These signals, even when merely incorporated in the bodily covering, may indicate species membership; with sexual maturity they may be transformed into mating adornment, or may serve as a warning to rivals. Visible pantomine may be used to indicate impressiveness or position in the social hierarchy.

2

The possibilities for variation through mechanical signals are the most diverse of all. Sound waves or vibrations may be presented in countless combinations and nuances. Their significance in communication is clear to every attentive observer, whether in the song of birds and grasshoppers or in the courting ceremony of the male spider.

Olfactory, optical, and mechanical signals are also employed for mutual communication in the bee society. The dance of the bee utilizes all three types of signal in a unique and unexcelled manner, by combining them for the symbolic transmission of information. It is not surprising that the problem of the phylogenetic development of this highly developed bee dance has been a source of lively interest to Professor von Frisch, the discoverer of the bees' language, from the very beginning. At first we searched in our own native bee societies for simple, elementary forms of communication, which might represent components of the bees' dance. Then we looked among related social bees for more primitive stages of the dance. We have also tried to exhaust the additional possibilities of meaning and details communicated in the bees' dance; and we have tried to investigate the physiology of those sensory mechanisms through which information is transferred.

Anyone who has ever looked into a beehive has surely asked himself, can there be any positive collaboration in that confusing, teeming mass of thousands of bees? But this collaboration must exist; otherwise the building of combs, the raising of brood, the collection and storing of food could never be carried out so regularly and harmoniously. And when we follow single bees through this confusion, by marking them with color spots, and observe their activities over a considerable period of time, we notice that every single one among them is going about a regulated task, as

Fig. 1. The poppy bee (*Osmia papaveris* Latr.) does all the work of
rearing young alone: the fertilized female digs a nest hole, cuts pieces

(*Continued on next page*)

if it had exact instructions about what to do at any time.

Our general question is: from where does the individual bee receive these instructions? Or, more generally: how do the bees communicate among themselves in order to achieve such a harmonious collaboration?

Up to the present we have information about only a few aspects of mutual communication in the beehive. What I can report on deals with communication concerning the division of labor, the temperature regulation in the hive, the collecting of food, and the search for housing.

~ Communication Concerning Division of Labor ~

Division of labor was probably the first step leading from the hermit existence of the solitary bees to the foundation

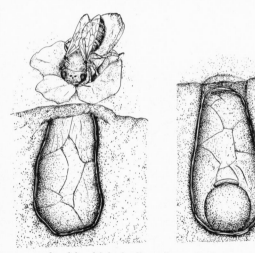

from flower petals with which she lines the walls, brings nectar and pollen to the nest and kneads it into a cake of fodder, lays an egg on this food ball, closes the nest, and then disappears, never to see her offspring.

5

of a social organization. Most relatives of our honeybee live a solitary life. Take for example the poppy bee (Fig. 1); she digs all by herself a little hole in the earth, papers the walls with poppy petals, carries in a ball of food consisting of pollen and nectar, and finally places an egg on top of the ball. Then she closes the hole, and never returns to the spot. Likewise, in the *Dasypoda* and many other relatives like *Chalicodoma* and *Megachile,* there is no community life, although many breeding chambers are built in a row next to one another; for the mother will be dead when the young bees emerge from the pupae, and the young will scatter immediately in all directions.

Among these solitary bees, however, are some that show preliminary tendencies toward a social life. The basic condition for this appears to be that *the females are rather long-lived* and thus able to survive past the hatching of their brood. In *Halictus quadricinctus* (Fbr.), for example, or *H. marginatus* Brullé, the old female is still engaged in enlarging the nest and is still laying eggs in the newly built cells while her first offspring are already emerging. The young females do not fly away immediately to start a life of their own, but instead remain in the nest and join in enlarging it, collecting food and combining efforts to defend the parental home. A family community has thus emerged, in which each female still cares for her own offspring independently; but the joint nest-building activities and the combined defense constitute the first signs of communal activity.

In recent investigations C. Plateaux (1960) has found the very interesting fact that in *Halictus marginatus* Brullé the females keep continual contact with the larvae, leaving the brood cells open; furthermore, in this species the society develops more and more every year owing to the

6

production of several generations of workers in one nest. Only in the fourth or fifth summer the colony dies out when new females emerge, are fertilized, and then found a new nest—each one separately for herself—in the following spring.

We find significant progress toward the formation of a social community in *Augochloropsis sparsilis* (Vachal). Here the females remain together during the summer, and a regular division of labor is established among them. One can observe that some of them—the workers—are mainly or even exclusively occupied in collecting pollen and nectar, and building. Their colleagues are almost exclusively occu-

FIG. 2. A bumblebee nest (*Bombus hypnorum* L.). The queen nurses only the first dwarf workers to maturity; later she will receive more and more assistance from her female offspring in building, food gathering and care of brood, until finally she is able to devote herself entirely to egg laying. Here is shown the lumplike brood nest, and on the edge some storage cells filled with honey.

pied with egg laying. These latter bees, the queens, are morphologically basically identical with the worker bees, but one still can distinguish the two groups clearly by the fact that the workers have tattered wings and worn mandibles, whereas the queens appear fresh and well preserved. The distribution of labor appears to be accidental. It has been shown that many of the worker bees have never mated; for some reason, they returned from their nuptial flights unsuccessful. These unmated bees are now of great value for the community: they confine themselves to nest building and collecting activities, thus becoming specialists that free the fertile females for egg laying (Michener, 1958).

The next step toward a community life is represented by *Halictus malachurus* (Kirby), where the unmated workers are morphologically differentiated from the beginning. They are smaller than the fertile females, and thus the decisive step is made toward the simplest real insect community, the bumblebee colony (Fig. 2). Here the social life and with it the division of labor has become *obligatory*. The fertilized queen is actually still able to found a colony on her own, but she needs the collaboration of the smaller workers for the raising of sexually mature individuals.

In the honeybee community, the social structure and the division of labor have been developed to a high state of perfection. Not only is the queen differentiated from the worker bees; the worker bees among themselves have definite, specialized activities which they are obliged to perform. There are the *building bees,* which have to erect the comb structure. Hanging in closely packed assemblages, they secrete thin scales of wax from their abdominal wax glands, grasp the product with the wax tongs of their first legs, and with their mandibles knead and shape it piece by piece into the hexagonal comb cells (Fig. 3). Others are engaged in

8

FIG. 3. Construction of the honeybee comb is a communal activity of the building bees. They secrete tiny wax scales ventrally, knead them in their mandibles, and fit them together into these regular hexahedrons. (Photograph by E. Schuhmacher.)

repairs on older nest structure; they remove old wax from unused areas and use it to close the breeding cells or mend damaged comb structures.

The *brood nurses* are always engaged in inspecting larvae in the open cells (Fig. 4). They give the larvae food composed of honey and pollen, and let the secretion product of their nurse glands run onto the floor of the cells, where the larvae can pick it up. Other bees are entrusted with *cleaning;* they must prepare the empty cells for egg deposit, by cleaning them and lining them with a lacquerlike substance. They also must remove waste from the nest. In addition, one finds the *honey makers,* who make the honey by evaporating the nectar and splitting its sucrose into dextrose and

Fig. 4. The "nursery" of a beehive: *(above)* egg and day-old larva in brood cells; *(below)* cell cleaners and brood nurses at work. (Photograph by E. Schuhmacher.)

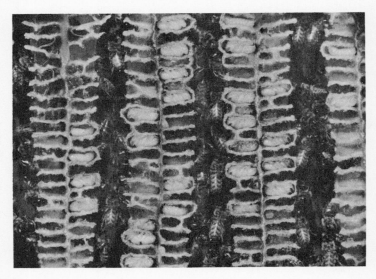

F<small>IG</small>. 5. Guard bees on duty at the entrance of the hive. (Photograph by Harald Doering.)

levulose. The *pollen stampers* compress the stripped pollen loads in the cells, for storage. The *guard bees* stand at their posts at the nest entrance (Fig. 5), and the large army of *pollen and nectar collectors* cares for the food supply of the hive (Figs. 6 and 7).

From these observations one might conclude that every bee from youth on specializes in a particular function, whether as nurse or as builder or as forager. But this is not so. Every worker bee performs in succession each of the various tasks necessary to the bees' community. In doing so, the individual bees follow a schedule, so to speak, which prescribes their obligations according to age (Fig. 8). Immediately after emergence, the young bee is engaged in cleaning cells for about three days; then she is detached to the nurse contingent. From about the tenth to the sixteenth day of her life she is a builder; then, for a few days, she

Fig. 6. A forager bee pocketing the pollen. She has collected pollen from pussy willows in her hairy coat and now—during the flight—she combs it from her hair and compresses it into the little pockets on her hind legs. (Photograph by E. Schuhmacher.)

undertakes the reception of nectar and the storage of pollen. Around the twentieth day she can be seen standing guard at the entrance of the hive; and from the third week until the end of her life she works as a forager bee out in the field.

It may appear from this schedule as if there were no need for mutual communication about the division of labor—as if everything were automatically regulated according to the bees' age. This impression has been strengthened in view of the fact that the various occupations of the worker bees are synchronized with the development of their nursing or wax glands. The nursing glands are most highly developed from the fifth to the tenth day, and the wax glands from the tenth to the eighteenth day (Fig. 8). After that time the

FIG. 7. A nectar gatherer. (Photograph by Harald Doering.)

13

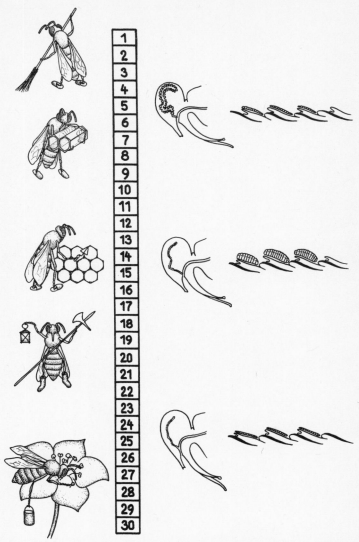

FIG. 8. The schedule of a worker bee, arranged on the basis of her age in days. Her activity at a given time is correlated with the development of the nurse glands (in the head) and the wax glands (ventral in the abdomen).

14

secretions of these two glands stop completely (Rösch, 1925, 1927, 1930).

This preliminary finding, however, was not quite satisfactory. Supply and demand are by no means always balanced in the bees' community. They are dependent on weather, the richness of the harvest, and the age of the queen. Sometimes there are more larvae to be nursed, sometimes fewer. After a prolonged period of bad weather, there may suddenly be a good harvest, and then it is important to have as many foragers available as possible for collecting it. At other times, there may be insufficient storage space for the honey; then additional builder bees are required for speedy enlargement of storage space. Are such irregularities, which could severely disturb the harmony of the bees' social organization, simply accepted? Or is there some provision to insure that every day, at each working place, the appropriate number of workers will appear?

A first experiment on this question was performed by Rösch (1930). He tried to confuse the labor market in a bees' community through artificial interference. He deprived one colony of all nursing bees, and another of all forager bees. That can easily be done by displacing the hive by a few meters and setting up a new hive on the old location, a hive without bees but with combs and a queen in a wire cage. The old foragers who are accustomed to the terrain will start from the parent hive and return to the starting point that they had previously learned. In this way, after a few hours, the older bees will be populating the new hive at the old location, and the parent hive will have been deprived of all older foragers. We have now formed two colonies, consisting of two age groups, one composed of young bees, the other of old field bees. Could both these new

communities survive this critical situation, where one population lacked young nurses, the other lacked old collectors?

It was found that in the old population those bees which
still felt somewhat young were soon indulging themselves
in the pollen and honey larders; they became fat, regener-
ated their nursing glands, and carried on nursing again,
although they were long past the nursing age. For the young
population, however, the experiment seemed to result in
catastrophe. By the second day the food was all gone, and
a few bees were already lying on the ground, dead of star-
vation. But none of the young, inexperienced bees was able
to collect the rich crop of food from the surrounding fields.
On the third day, however, the situation changed; a few
of the oldest bees ventured out into the country, and gradually more and more. They came back laden with nectar
and pollen, even though their well-developed head glands
marked them as still nursing bees, at most 8–12 days old.

Thus there did occur in the young population as well as
in the old a reorganization according to social demands,
which did not fit into the normal schedule of individual
development. Who led this striking reorganization? How
were the individual bees informed of the changed social
situation and what they had to do now?

To analyze this problem more fully, I considered it necessary to keep an individual bee under continuous observation, and under normal conditions, from the first day of her
life until her death. I built for this purpose a special observation hive (Fig. 9) which for the first time made possible
accurate observation of all activities, especially nursing.
Every activity of the marked bee was then recorded, day
and night, with the aid of a stopwatch. It was established
that even under normal conditions the division of labor was
not quite so rigid as had previously been supposed. On the

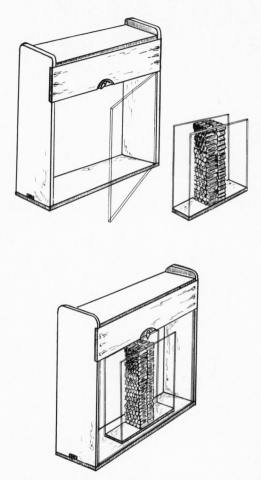

FIG. 9. A specially constructed observation box, which made possible exact observation especially of brood care. The bees were induced to build open brood cells on the glass wall. When this glass frame was then also placed behind glass, so that it was not cooled from outside, the rearing of the larvae progressed without difficulty. The double glass wall is necessary because the brood cells must be kept at a temperature of 34.5–35.5°C.

17

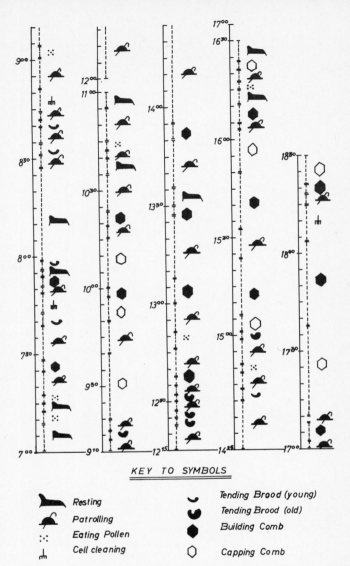

KEY TO SYMBOLS

	Resting		Tending Brood (young)
	Patrolling		Tending Brood (old)
	Eating Pollen		Building Comb
	Cell cleaning		Capping Comb

FIG. 10. A day's record of the activity of bee No. 107 on the eighth day of her life. The bee is not rigidly bound to brood care. When need arises, she can also participate in building activity and even cleaning duties. She is informed of the needs of the hive at any time by extended inspection tours.

whole, the bee does adhere to her schedule; but this can be readjusted to a large extent, and every bee can engage in other tasks in her spare time, depending on whether a working place happens to be vacant. It is this flexibility that guarantees the full harmony of the social life.

But now our first question becomes acute: how is the individual bee informed of what tasks need to be done at the moment?

This communication does not take place through specific orders passed on from one bee to another. A different and much simpler principle is applied here: every bee gathers *on her own* the necessary information about the current necessities within the hive. She does this by extensive patrolling around. Cells are inspected to see whether they are clean and prepared for egg laying; larvae are inspected to see if they are ready to be fed, other cells whether they are ready to be sealed. Seams and corners are searched for wastes, or the building areas are surveyed for needed construction work. Only for the field work are the hive bees actually recruited by a special alerting system. We shall learn more about this later.

An all-day record of bee number 107, taken on the eighth day of her life, shows clearly how much time is spent in patrolling (Fig. 10). One can see that every tour of inspection results in some form of activity: nursing once, building or cleaning on other occasions, just as the need arises. In a total of 177 hours over several days, this bee spent 56 hours on inspection tours (Lindauer, 1952).

Another thing is striking in this day's record: the bee spent a surprisingly large part of her life loafing. During 69 hours and 53 minutes of the total 177 observation hours, she just sat around, seeming lazy (Fig. 11). But if anyone thinks we should now revise our old ideas of the bee's

19

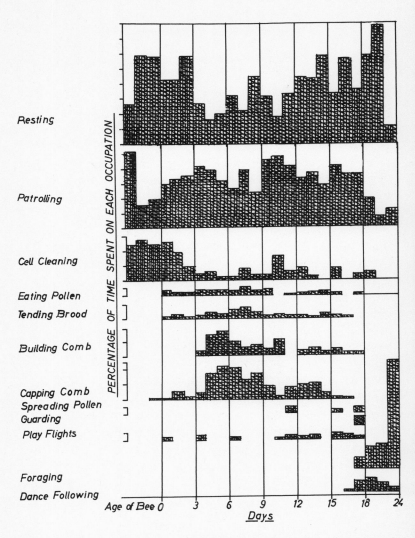

FIG. 11. The total work accomplished by bee No. 107 in the course of her life is here classified according to the type of work. One can recognize the age-determined succession of cell cleaning, brood care, building, guarding, and foraging; however, each of these activities can also be performed, as need arises, at other points in the bee's life. Note the large amount of time spent in patrolling and in seeming inactivity.

industry, they must be reminded that among the bees even laziness has an important social function. The loafers in the beehive are the reserve troops, employed at critical points in the labor market as the necessity arises. This is especially true for temperature regulation and food gathering (see following chapters).

Thus we have found in division of labor a simple method of spreading information. It is not a mutual communication from bee to bee; instead, each bee is its own informant and chief. This of course presupposes three requisites:

(*a*) A large repertoire of instinctive behavior patterns must be available; this is already present in the solitary bees, as we have mentioned before.

(*b*) There must be an absolutely socially directed drive, which can only develop as a result of degeneration of the ovaries of the worker bees; the workers have no drive for raising progeny of their own and thus direct all their building, nursing, and foraging instincts toward the social community.

(*c*) Finally, every bee has to be available for a community job at any moment, without the necessity for a direct summons from other bees. It is this state of alertness that is an important prerequisite for more highly developed means of communication, especially for a successful alerting mechanism like the bees' dance.

~ Communication
Concerning Temperature Regulation ~

Let me now point out a somewhat higher form of communication in connection with another social institution— communication in temperature regulation. The honeybees have developed temperature regulation to the highest

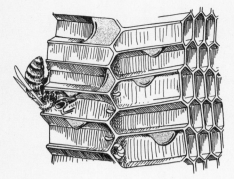

FIG. 12. When there is danger of overheating, drops of water are deposited in the cells. As the water evaporates, the surroundings are cooled. At the same time the other bees fan the moist air out of the hive. (After Park, 1925.)

degree found in any insect community. Although bees are poikilothermic individually, they maintain a constant temperature in the brood nest between 34.5° and 35.5°C, independent of outside temperature. Evidently they must have means at their command that enable them to heat or cool the hive, and this can be done only in social collaboration. The bees produce warmth by clustering together over the brood nest and generating heat through muscle vibrations; thus they cover the brood cells like a warm, living blanket.

The methods used for cooling are more complicated. When it becomes too warm, the bees first cool by fanning. When the temperature outside the hive rises above, say, 34°C, fanning alone is not enough. The principle of water evaporation is now used for cooling purposes. Water is carried into the hive and distributed on the cells in tiny droplets (Fig. 12). Droplets are deposited particularly at the entrances of the open brood cells. At the same time a large number of bees can be seen hanging over the brood cells and continuously extending their proboscises back and forth. Each time they do this they press a drop of water from their mouths and spread it with the proboscis into a film, which has a large evaporating surface (Fig. 13). When the water evaporates, the proboscis is retracted again and a new droplet is spread out. (Many years ago Park (1925)

22

found that the same method is used for nectar concentrating.) The cooling effect achieved by this method is amazing. On a lava field in southern Italy, near Salerno, I exposed a hive of bees to full sunlight at more than 70°C. Even there, the temperature within the hive remained at a constant 35°C as long as I provided water from a nearby bee's drinking fountain (Lindauer, 1954). This temperature regulation within the hive demands a very precise collaboration between the water collectors, who bring in the water from outside, and the water spreaders, who distribute it in the hive for evaporation.

One should keep in mind that the situation here is quite different from the nectar collecting, as water cannot be brought in indefinitely. Water cannot be stored as nectar can, and as soon as the overheating is past water collecting must cease. It cannot start too late, either, otherwise, temperature regulation would break down immediately.

One might imagine that each bee would set out to collect water as soon as it detects the overheating. This is not so; not just any bee is able to collect water. Only bees that

FIG. 13. In addition to water distribution, proboscidal agitation also serves in temperature regulation. Water drops are rhythmically extruded from the mouth, then drawn out by the proboscis to a thin film, which presents a large surface for evaporation. Thousands of hive bees simultaneously participate in this activity when there is danger of overheating. (After Park, 1925.)

know the terrain and are experienced foragers can perform this task. Furthermore, it is an advantage when bees are divided into water collectors and water sprinklers. So there is a very strict division of labor between the older flying bees, who collect water outside, and the younger hive bees, who distribute it. Indeed, we found a special mode of communication by means of which the water collectors receive instructions from the hive bees about when to start collecting and when to stop.

Let us begin with the simple case. Let us assume that water collecting is still in progress and the foragers are to be informed whether or not there is need for more water. To transmit this information the hive bees make use of *the short moment when they have contact with the collectors;* this is during water delivery at the entrance hole. As long as overheating exists, the home-coming foragers are relieved of their burdens with great greed; three or four bees at once may rush up to a collector and suck from her the extruded water droplet. This stormy begging informs the collector bee that there is a pressing need for more water. When the overheating begins to subside, however, the hive bees show less interest in the water collectors. The latter now have to run around in the hive themselves, trying to find somewhere a bee that will relieve them of at least part of the water load. The delivery in such cases takes much more time, of course. This rejecting attitude contains the message "Water needs fulfilled," and the water collecting will thus stop, even though the collectors themselves have not been at the brood nests to experience the changed temperature situation.

This delivery time is in fact an accurate gauge of water demand. As shown in Fig. 14, with delivery times of up to 60 sec, the collecting is continued industriously. Beyond that, however, the eagerness for collecting decreases rapidly, and when delivery takes longer than 3 min collecting practically ceases altogether.

A second point is apparent from Fig. 14: when delivery times are very short (up to 40 sec), the water collectors even perform recruiting dances to stimulate hive bees to fly to the water source. As we shall see in the next chapter, it is possible by such means to recruit helpers, who will then also fly out and collect the necessary water. These recruiting dances subside somewhat if the delivery time is longer than 40 sec, and later cease completely.

I should point out in this connection what a high social achievement is represented by the bee that collects water instead of sugar water. As flower visitors, the bees have a natural craving for sweets. At an artificial feeding place, under normal conditions, one can easily estrange a collector

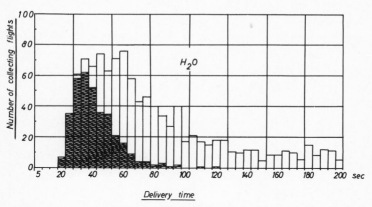

FIG. 14. A need for water is communicated to the forager bees by the receiving hive bees: the more quickly water is accepted by the hive bees, the more diligently will the forager bees collect more water. The number of water-collecting flights decreases as the time required for delivery increases. With very short delivery times (20–40 sec; *shaded columns*), the foraging bees are even induced to perform an alerting dance after each collecting flight, to recruit new bees to help gather water.

bee if one offers her 1-molar instead of 2-molar sugar water. Even so, it is a perfectly social attitude, because if too watery nectar were delivered the hive bees would have too much difficulty in thickening it, and the honey would be more perishable. If, however, the social need calls for water, one can observe the same sweet-craving bees transformed into water collectors. Now the 1-molar sugar solution is accepted, as well as ½-molar, and even pure water. During an over-heating experiment, I once offered a choice between 2-molar sugar solution and pure water, and I was very much impressed to see that these bees would then always prefer the water. Sometimes they would let themselves be tempted into taking a sweet drink, but after they experienced rejecting attitudes of the receiving bees at the hive, these same bees would visit the water vessel on their next flight. The subjective desire for a sweet drink and the satisfaction that a collector normally derives from it are thus suppressed in favor of the social needs of the community. We must marvel at the fact that it is simply the attitude of the recipient bees which regulates the future food choice in such a way as to be best for the community.

So far we have avoided the most difficult problem in connection with the communication about temperature regulation: how is the *first* water forager notified that she should start on a water-collection flight? The first information that there is a water shortage in the hive cannot come from the receiving bees. If one creates a water shortage in the hive by means of a sudden overheating, at a time when not a single bee is occupied as a water forager, the communication indeed seems to fail at first, for no bee appears at the water dish. And still the temperature-regulation system does not collapse. The hive bees (that is, the water sprinklers), being too young to be able to collect water them-

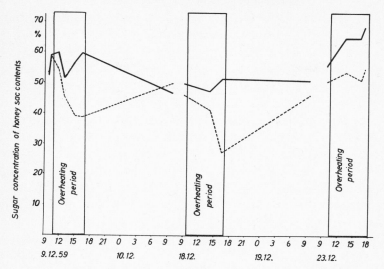

FIG. 15. Three overheating experiments. When overheating threatens, the total water reserve shifts to the brood nest in the middle of the hive, whereas at the periphery the sugar concentration in the honey stomachs remains the same or is even increased. In the experiments on 9.12 and 18.12, the water carriers could bring water to the hive from the drinking fountains provided; in the experiment on 23.12, the fountains were removed. *Solid line:* bees in the vicinity of the flight entrance; *broken line:* bees from the brood nests.

selves, take an emergency measure: they use the contents of their own honey stomachs, which they carry around with them as a feeding reserve, as a substitute for water. As we could show by our own measurements, the honey stomach of the hive bees does not contain pure concentrated honey, but a nutritious solution that is about 60 percent water. Through regurgitation, they now distribute water-containing droplets, and improve evaporation of the water contents of the honey stomach by agitating it with their proboscises. As a result of this, in a few minutes all bees in the region of overheating have only a highly concentrated sugar solution left in their honey stomachs. One can observe now that *a mutual begging starts, which spreads from the center of overheating to the periphery;* by means of a characteristic stretching out of their proboscises and tapping movements of their antennas, the water sprinklers demand from their colleagues at the periphery an exchange of the contents of their own honey stomachs—and the latter indeed obey this summons.

In this remarkable way, the whole reserve of water-containing fluid moves into the center of the hive, while at the same time the sugar concentration at the periphery is increased (Kiechle, unpublished) (Fig. 15). Within a short time, however, the last water reserves are used up and the begging for water is concentrated more and more around

FIG. 16. A group of marked forager bees were fed during an entire summer at an artificial feeding place, where sugar water was offered in just such a concentration that the forager bees would perform recruiting dances back in the hive. At times when the natural harvests offered strong competition, highly concentrated sugar water had to be offered; when the harvest was lean, the bees were satisfied with weak sugar solutions and performed the same excited recruiting dances as they formerly had in May when 2-molar sugar solution was offered. By means of the behavior of the bees who relieve them of their loads at the flight entrance, the foragers are informed of requirements inside the hive.

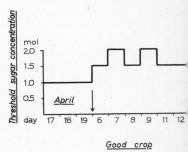

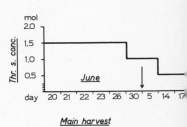

28

the flight hole where the nectar collectors arrive. In contrast to the usual situation, the collectors most in demand are now those that carry a "low-quality" food, one that contains relatively more water; highly concentrated nectar is rejected or accepted only hesitantly. Thus the nectar collectors are informed of the increasing need for water, and some of them—these are the pioneers of the beehive— cease collecting nectar and appear at the water dish; they have become water foragers. Thus the situation is saved, although after a certain lag. Instigated by the stormy begging of the hive bees, the first water foragers will recruit newcomers through dances, and within a short time the necessary amount of water will be at hand.

Without doubt this method of communication in temperature regulation is still a very simple one, but it clearly

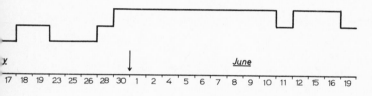

Main harvest

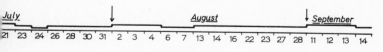

No crop

29

is at a higher level than that described in connection with the division of labor; it is really a *mutual communication* whereby the begging bee gives both distinct *information* about the social demands and a strict *order* to continue or to cease collecting water.

~ Conclusion ~

We found two elementary means of communication within the bees' community:

(1) The reconnaissance (patrolling) tours of the individual bees, which always lead to a social activity and insure communication of social needs concerning the division of labor;

(2) The mutual begging and food transmission as a means for regulating water supply.

I should mention that this means of communication—namely, begging and food transmission—has a much higher importance in the social life of bees than one might assume at first. Not only the water demand for temperature regulation is reported in this way, but also the water needs *of the brood nurses,* which must prepare the liquid food for nursing the larvae. This explains the heavy water demand of the bee community in spring, for in winter they depended entirely on highly concentrated honey stocks.

Not only is the water gathering regulated by mutual food-transmission. This method also informs the various groups of foragers every day about the best source of nectar one of them might have found. Foragers coming from relatively inferior food sources have a hard time getting rid of their food in the hive, and thus the whole collecting force is finally directed toward the best food source available at the moment (Fig. 16).

The high social importance of food transmission is not confined to the bees, but also occurs in ants and termites, as Wilson (1956, 1957) and Lüscher (1955, 1958) have reported recently. We may expect to hear more about the high social function of this primitive form of communication in the future.

2

Communication by Dancing in Swarm Bees

LIKE THE DIVISION OF LABOR and the regulation of temperature, so also the search for food and the seeking of a dwelling represent most important life problems for a bee community. However, the demands on mutual communication are far greater and the modes are more specialized in the seeking of food and housing than those of which we learned in the last chapter.

~ Communication by Means of Dances in the Search for Food ~

For the bee community it is a problem of vital importance that newly discovered sources of crops be exploited as quickly as possible, before the blossoms close their calyces and before competing bee populations take away the newly found nectar. A special highly developed recruiting system assures this quick exploitation. Since Professor von Frisch some years ago reported on the language of the bees (von

HARVARD BOOKS IN BIOLOGY

NUMBER 2

COMMUNICATION AMONG SOCIAL BEES

Frisch 1950), I shall keep my discussion of this subject rather brief.

If a worker bee has found a good source of food, she announces her discovery at home by means of either a "round dance" or a "tail-wagging dance." If the food is to be found less than 80 meters away, she performs a *round dance,* running around rapidly in a circle, first to the left, then to the right, and the surrounding bees become excited by this dance. They follow interestedly behind the dancer and thus receive the message: "Fly out from the hive; right in the neighborhood is food to be fetched." The smell of the blossoms still remaining on the dancers gives the further information how the food source smells, and in this way the informed seekers can hunt out the fragrant blossoms.

If, however, the food source is a good distance away, then the *tail-wagging dance* gives additional information about the exact location of the newly discovered goal. The rhythm of this dance shows the distance: the farther away the goal, the fewer cycles of the dance in a given time. When the goal is close, there are more turns per minute. The direction of the goal is also conveyed by the tail-wagging part of the dance, the sun being used as a reference point. On the vertical honeycomb in the dark beehive the angle between the direction to the sun and that to the food source is transposed into an angle with respect to gravity, according to the following rule: a tail-wagging run pointed upward means that the source of food lies in the direction of the sun; the same part of the dance directed downward announces that the food is opposite to the sun. If the tail-wagging run points 60° left of straight up, the food source is 60° to the left of the sun, and so on (Fig. 17).

These soliciting dances last only as long as the food is in abundance, and only first class, highly concentrated nectar solutions are advertised. The quality of each source of food can be seen from the duration and vivacity of the dance. Since the number of newly won followers is dependent on the same factors, these dances harmonize supply and demand in the search for food in an almost perfect manner.

∼ Communication by Means of Dances in the Search for a Dwelling ∼

It has become known only in the last few years that these dances of the bees not only serve to give information in the search for food, but also play a decisive role in mutual communication during the search for a dwelling. There is no doubt that, next to the search for food, this presents one of of the most important problems of existence in a bee community.

The home of the bees must not only offer protection and shelter from cold, wind, and rain, it must not only be a

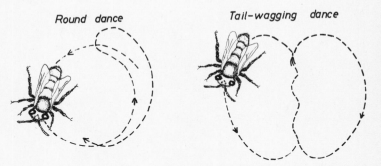

Round dance   Tail-wagging dance

FIG. 17. Patterns for the round and tail-wagging dances. The round dance, for short distances to a food source, announces no direction or distance. Information on both direction and distance are included in the pattern of the tail-wagging dance. The direction of the tail-wagging run (*middle wavy line*) conveys the direction to the goal, while the rhythm of the dance—that is the number of these tail-wagging runs per unit of time —communicates the distance. (After von Frisch, 1954.)

34

nursery for the growing brood, but it must also serve as a point of departure in the search for nourishment, from which the forager bees can easily exploit the surrounding feeding places. Most important of all, it must offer a central meeting place, where all individuals of the social community can come together again and again and coordinate their activities in useful teamwork. It is therefore understandable that mutual communication in the seeking of a dwelling is of special importance.

Under natural conditions, a population of bees can often retain its ancestral home for years and generations. However, every year in May or June such a large increase in offspring occurs that soon the space in the parental dwelling is no longer sufficient for the growing number of larvae and for the stream of nectar and pollen from the richly flowing sources of nourishment. The bees take care of this situation, brought about by reproduction, by dividing the original population; that is to say, they establish a new community. Such a division is prepared for long in advance. The young queens are quite early given the prerogative, and, even before the first has emerged as an adult (Fig. 18), the old mother of the hive moves out with about half of the bees and sets up a dwelling in another location. She thereby leaves house, honeycomb, and food supplies behind for her successors—the strongest of whom takes over after defeating the others in duels—and presents herself and her following with the difficult problem of house hunting and the establishment of a new home.

Swarming is the name given to this phenomenon, which we are unfortunately never able to follow in detail up to the very end. The beekeeper saves his bees the trouble of seeking a dwelling, as he hurries to enclose the swarming cluster in an empty box; he places honeycombs at the dis-

FIG. 18. The young queen emerges from the queen cell. She will be the successor of the old mother, who now leaves the hive with the swarm. (Photograph by Harald Doering.)

FIG. 19. After moving out from the mother hive the swarming cloud of bees first forms a cluster in the immediate neighborhood of the hive. (Photograph by E. Schumacher.)

posal of the young population and takes care that they start the winter with an abundance of provisions. However, bees existed long before human beings, and it can often happen that a swarm leaves behind the protection of the beekeeper and flies back into the forests, where its ancestors lived. Here the bees must see to their living quarters for themselves, and we shall now accompany them in their search for a dwelling.

Scout bees announce the location of suitable nesting places by means of the dance in the cluster

Very soon after the swarming bees have assembled themselves in a cluster (Fig. 19), scouts fly out in all directions to find suitable nesting places. After a short time some of them come back and announce a newly found spot. Like successful forager bees, they make known the location of the goal by means of the tail-wagging dance, in which again the rhythm of the dance shows the distance of the place, its direction being indicated by the direction of the tail-wagging run. Many bees in the cluster are aroused by the dance; they fly off and inspect the spot indicated, return to the cluster, and take part in announcing the location with a dance.

As I observed such dances in the cluster for the first time, I was of the opinion that the dancers were the normal nectar or pollen collectors, which provide the swarm bees with food. On closer observation, however, it struck me that these dancers never brought home loads of pollen and that they never delivered nectar. Therefore they were definitely not forager bees. In order to make sure of this, we marked the dancers with paint spots, then took down their announcement of location with stopwatch and compass, marked the place shown on an ordnance-survey map, and set about to find this spot. This we were able to do in a few cases, and we convinced ourselves that no forager bees were at work, but rather house hunters. We found the marked bees again, but they took no interest in blossoms or sweet sources of nectar; on the contrary, they busily inspected holes in the ground, hollows of trees, or a crack in an old wall, during which activity they not only checked the cavities themselves by repeatedly flying into them, but also examined the surrounding territory. Soon other bees arrived, which were apparently recruited by the dances, and they performed the same inspection flights at the future nesting place.

Here I would like to add a short note. Some people who hear about the dance of the bees for the first time may be skeptical about the possibility of the bees' being able to communicate, by means of symbols, such exact information concerning the location of a small spot somewhere in the outdoors. However, there is no better proof for the correctness of the interpretation of the dance of the bees, as it has been given by Professor von Frisch, and that we correctly understand the language of the bees, than the experiment just described. The nesting place was completely unknown to us beforehand, for the scouting bees had chosen it themselves. We were able only to observe the dancing bees in the swarm and to decide from their behavior the location of what they had found. We did not follow the swarm as it moved into its new dwelling; we were there at the future nesting place hours before its arrival.

Before moving, the swarm agrees
upon one of the nesting places offered

If one follows for some time the dances of the scouting bees in the cluster and records their announcements of location, one comes to a very surprising conclusion: not just one nesting place is reported, but rather announcements are given of different directions and distances, and this means that several possible dwellings are announced at the same time. For example: on 27 June 1952 I noticed a dance in a cluster, which reported a nesting place 300 meters to the south. A few minutes later a second dance could be observed which announced another nesting site 1400 meters to the east. In the next 2 hours, five more announcements came in, from the northeast, north, and northwest, with varied reports of distance, and by evening of the same day an eighth announcement, of a spot 1100 meters to the southeast, had to be booked. On the next day 14 new reports of locations of nesting places were added, so that now there were 21 different possibilities to choose from. The scout bees showed at the first glance that they had inspected various quarters: some were powdered over with dried dirt, because they had burrowed in a hole in the ground; others came from a cave in a ruin and were covered with red brick dust; once these seekers of quarters were soiled with soot, having discovered a suitable nesting place in a narrow chimney that was not in use during the summer. We now have to answer the difficult question how agreement is reached in the cluster about which of the nesting places offered should be chosen. Only one of them can be selected, for the entire swarm must move with its queen and cannot split itself up into small groups.

First of all we wish to investigate whether such agreement really takes place, and later solve the problem of how it comes about. We were struck by the fact that the swarm remained often for days, sometimes even 1 to 2 weeks, at its first landing place, after which delay it then moved to the new dwelling. This was also the case when a thunderstorm came up in the evening or a period of rain set in. The moving was therefore not undertaken prematurely; rather, some agreement had to be reached before the swarm moved to the new dwelling. This was concluded from the following observation. During the first hours and days after the flying out of the swarm, one saw the dancers in the cluster dancing in different directions. As now a continuous record of the number and kind of these dances was kept, it could be established that these dances gradually became more unified. A definite direction and distance came to be preferred, while dances for other territories were little by little given up. This went so far that we could finally record a dozen scouting bees doing the same kind of dance at the same time, and this meant nothing else but that they were

40

advertising in unison the same goal. Only when the good fortune of agreement finally came about was the sign given to fly off, and the swarm moved out in the announced direction.

Figure 20 shows what such a record looks like. Each dancer was marked with a spot of paint and its announcement entered in the record book. Each arrow indicates a new dancer; the direction and length of the arrow show to scale the location of the reported goal. Twenty-one nesting places were discovered by the scouting bees of this swarm. During the first 3 days no sign of agreement could be recognized. In the best case one could assume that the nesting place 3 kilometers to the north was given some preference. Not until the fourth day was an increasing interest shown in the nesting place 350 meters to the south-east; dwelling sites in another region were still advertised, but these announcements disappeared more and more, until southeast triumphed with an overwhelming majority. Finally, on the fifth day, after all competitors had been silenced and an agreement had been reached, the swarming ceased and the bees flew off together to the southeast. We were able to follow the swarm, and it actually alighted on the ruins of a wall 350 meters away and there moved into a hollow space (Fig. 21). For years we could still see the bees flying in and out, until the wall was finally torn down. From all appearances the scouting bees had chosen a suitable nesting site.

I must however confess that agreement in the swarming cluster is not always reached so smoothly and with so little friction as has just been described. It often happens that interest is divided equally and at the same time between two nesting places. In such a case it is always very difficult to force one of the two groups to surrender. Figure 22 pictures this tug-of-war among the scouting bees. Also,

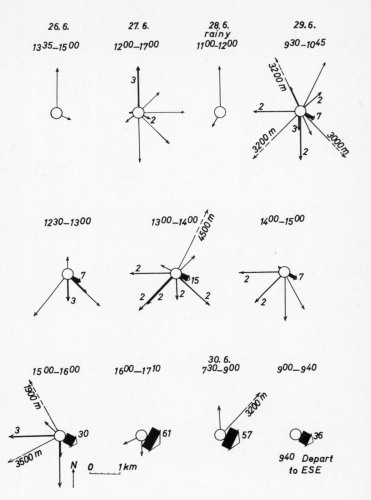

FIG. 20. Example of the recorded announcements of the scouting bees from the moment of swarming at 13:35 on 26 June until the moving into the new dwelling at 9:40 on 30 June. Each arrow represents a newly marked scouting bee that announced a nesting place by means of a dance in the cluster. Direction and length of the arrow give to scale the location of the reported nesting place. First of all nesting places in different directions and distances are announced, but gradually an agreement is reached for the nesting place 350 meters to the southeast.

FIG. 21. The nesting place (*circle*) of the swarm described in Fig. 20, which we had discovered before the swarm moved in, only by questioning the dancing scouting bees.

three or four groups of equal size can compete with one another. Still an agreement must always be reached before the swarm flies off. We have watched 19 swarms of bees from the moment that they moved out of the hive until they moved into the new dwelling decided upon by the swarming cluster. Only twice did we observe that no agreement was reached. Such a thing, however, would have soon led to a catastrophe.

In the first case two groups of messengers had got into competition; one group announced a nesting place to the northwest, the other one to the northeast. Neither of the two

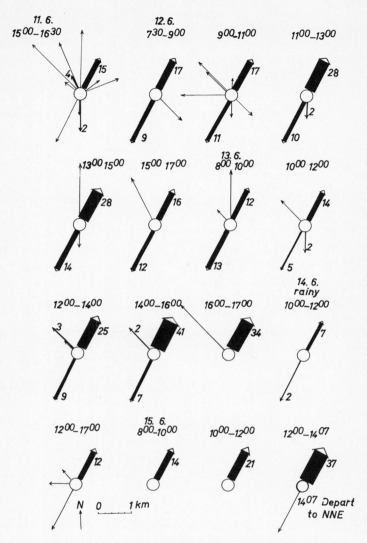

FIG. 22. It may happen that two equally strong groups of scouting bees enter into competition with one another. Then an agreement appears to offer special difficulties. But in this case also the move takes place only when one of the groups has given up its soliciting.

44

wished to yield. The swarm then finally flew off and I could scarcely believe my eyes—it sought to divide itself. The one half wanted to fly to the northwest, the other to the northeast. Apparently each group of scouting bees wanted to abduct the swarm to the nesting place of its own choice. But that was naturally not possible, for one group was always without the queen, and there resulted a remarkable tug of war in the air, once 100 meters to the northwest, then again 150 meters to the northeast, until finally after half an hour the swarm gathered together at the old location. Immediately both groups began again with their soliciting dances, and it was not until the next day that the northeast group finally yielded; they ended their dance and thus an agreement was reached on the nesting place in the northwest.

The second case ended in a completely unexpected way; for 14 days no agreement had been reached, and then, when a period of rain set in, the scouting bees gave up their search for a dwelling and occupied themselves instead with the collection of nectar and pollen. The traveling stores of the swarm bees were apparently used up and it was high time for a replacement of provisions. Thus the activity of the hunters of quarters was completely suppressed, and the swarm made its abode at its first landing place, built honeycombs in the bushes, and set up a normal nest for its brood (Fig. 23). We must view this as the last emergency measure of the swarm, which makes possible its further existence when the scouting bees occasionally fail in their task. In our climatic region the winter would put an end to this attempt, for the bees cannot survive a heavy frost in the open. However, the ancestral home of our bees was southeast Asia; there it is entirely possible, even as a freely living cluster, for them to endure an entire year. The nearest relatives of our European bees, *Apis florea* and *A. dorsata* (the dwarf

honeybees and the giant honeybees), still nest only in the open. Our native bees have retained this living habit of these Indian bees, so to say as their last lifesaver, when the search for a dwelling is unsuccessful.

~ Agreement Is on the Best of the Nesting Places Offered ~

When the swarming bees do not come to an agreement, as in the case just described, this is a rare exception. Our next question will therefore be: *how* does this agreement come about? We wish to recall the situation again clearly; the swarm hovers on a tree unprotected and without possibility of shelter, and now 20 or more dwellings are offered. Who makes the decision? Upon what aspects will the decision depend? To make one thing clear at the beginning, the queen has no say in the matter. In several experiments I placed her in a single or double wire cage, so that she could in no way come in contact with the dancers, and nevertheless agreement was reached. The swarm flew off, and only when in the air did it become aware that the queen was missing; then it gathered together again around the cage. If the queen was now set free, the move took place without further ado. Therefore the *worker bees* must make the decision. It must, however, be realized that they are 10,000 to 30,000 in number. Which of them shall decide which nesting place should be chosen? Can each separate bee influence the decision, or is it the affair of a small committee, whose decision all other bees of the swarm accept without question?

It seemed almost obvious that the house hunters themselves would make the decision, and the following observation gave the first clue to how an agreement could be reached. When once again all the dancing scouts were marked, it struck me that those dancers which the day before had solicited for the southeast, today announced a nesting place in the north. This was the nesting site that was already preferred by most of the other dancers. Had the former allowed themselves to be brought around for another nesting place? It was conceivable that they had let themselves be persuaded by the dancers from the north, and that they had then inspected this second nesting place, and now joined in soliciting for it in the cluster, perhaps because it was the better dwelling site. In any case, we arrived at the following conclusions: (1) the decision concerning the choice of a nesting place lies solely with the scouting bees; (2) the choice is always for the best nesting place offered.

For the sake of clarity, I should first mention that the dancers in the cluster give information not only concerning the *location* of the new dwelling place, but also concerning

47

its *quality*. The location is announced by the direction of the tail-wagging run and by the rhythm of the dance, the quality by the liveliness and the duration of the dance. By this is meant that a dance for an inferior dwelling place is performed quite sluggishly. This is indeed a subjective characteristic, but so striking that any layman can differentiate a sluggish from a lively dance. Moreover, it can be established that a sluggish dance always has fewer bees as dance followers than a lively one, and it is broken up after a few seconds. A lively dance, which has a highly qualified dwelling to announce, can last many minutes, even hours, and it is obvious that thereby many more newcomers become alerted and informed than by a dance of short duration. Very soon more messengers will go to the better nesting place, and when they solicit for this site in the same way the interest in it will become more and more concentrated. Whether all this definitely corresponds to the facts could not be established by observations of the swarming cluster alone. We also had to find out what took place at the different nesting places before the move to one of them. Artificial nesting sites had to be used, and artificial changes had to be made in the future home of the bees, in order to establish the basic causes of the agreement.

I then tried to offer my scouting bees artificial nesting places. In order to hinder the competition with natural nesting places as far as possible, we placed our swarm on an uninhabited island or in a broad, wide waste land, where the house hunters had no chance to find natural holes, hollow trees, or the like. And so we hoped that our artificially erected breeding cages would be accepted.

In the first experiment two boxes of the same size were set up in an uncultivated field; in order to make them of different worth to the scouting bees, the first box (*A*) was placed under a bush for protection and covered with twigs, while the other (*B*) stood completely free in the open field. A few days earlier we had assembled an artificial swarm, and this we let form a cluster at the same distance from both nesting boxes, by shaking the bees out freely on the ground. Both nesting places were found and inspected by the messengers and reported by dances in the cluster. One could see by the liveliness of the dances that the two boxes were of very different quality, although the scouting bees that had sought out nesting place *B* knew nothing about the competition from *A*. They announced their finding through but a faint-hearted dance, while the other group, which came from the bush, solicited with a lively and long-lasting dance. The consequence was that within a short time many more new messengers visited the bush than the free standing nesting box, and also that more dancers solicited for this nesting place in the cluster. Now it could be observed beyond a doubt that those marked scouting bees which had danced first for the unprotected spot let themselves be solicited by the lively dances of their competitive group into also inspecting the second place. After the inspection they too solicited with their dances for this better nesting place. They had therefore let their minds be changed.

It was definitely the protected location that was decisive in the evaluation of the scouting bees; shortly before agreement was final, and the move was to be expected in a few minutes, we took the protective covering of twigs and the artificial bush away from nesting place *A* and transposed them to nesting place *B*. All at once the picture was changed; the few inspecting bees that had still remained by *B* flew back excitedly to the cluster and performed now most lively dances, while the scouting bees from *A* little by little ended their dance. Spot *A* became deserted and at *B* a new concourse took place very rapidly. By such a transposition we could dispel the unity of the swarms as often as we pleased, and could finally let the swarm move into which ever one of these nesting places we wished. It was always the protected place that the bees chose for their dwelling.

Thus the agreement appears to take place in a seemingly simple manner; the better the qualities a nesting place exhibits, the livelier and longer will be the messengers' dance after the inspection. In this way new messengers are recruited in the cluster for this place, which then likewise seek out and inspect this nesting place, and then they too solicit by means of the same lively dances. If those scouting bees which at first had only inferior or average dwellings to announce are persuaded by the livelier dances of their colleagues to inspect the other nesting place, then nothing more stands in the way of an agreement. They can now make a comparison between their own and the new nesting place, and they will solicit in the cluster for the better of the two.

Thus we have arrived at a new problem. It is not just the protected location of the bees' dwelling that determines it as a suitable place for living. A number of other characteristics must be considered, and all of them together will influence the final judgment of the scouting bee. Therefore we now ask, how can the scouting bees judge so exactly the quality of a nesting place? How many and what characteristics of a dwelling for the bees are considered? Which are positively, which negatively valued?

~ How the Scouting Bees
Judge the Quality of a Nesting Place ~

First of all we sought purely empirically to offer the bees

some characteristics of a nesting place for their judgment. We have just mentioned that the location of the future dwelling plays an important role, and it is chiefly, according to the long experience of beekeepers, protection against wind that must be taken into account. The wind however, can change from day to day; on the day of swarming an east wind might prevail, and the nesting place might be screened toward the east. Then after the swarm has moved in, the wind might easily shift to the west and possibly make the nesting place worthless. It seems particularly noteworthy that the scouting bees take into calculation such changeable factors in their search for a dwelling. They do not just visit the nesting place once and let themselves be satisfied with the first inspection, but rather they come back after an hour or two, and again on the next day and likewise on the days following, until the move is decided upon. In this way they can assure themselves whether the chosen nesting place retains its qualities unchanged over a considerable period of time, or whether something has eventually changed to its disadvantage. If this is the case, they immediately abandon their first position and let themselves be solicited by other dancers for the inspection of a better nesting place.

Here is an example. A swarm was offered two nesting places, in our opinion of exactly the same worth. Both stood protected on the edge of a wood, the only difference being that the one had open land to the west, the other to the east (Fig. 24). The debate in the cluster lasted 6 days until agreement was reached. On those days when a west wind prevailed, that nesting place was preferred which had the wood behind it to the west, but with an east wind the second place was favored. Because, however, during the final days a lasting west wind set in, the swarm finally moved into the nesting place protected from the west.

51

FIG. 24. Here an artificial nesting place was set up at the edge of a wood, in such a position that it had open land to the east but was protected from the west. On days with a west wind this place was preferred to a second one, which was open to the west. On days with an east wind, however, the scouting bees showed less interest in it.

Another time agreement was almost reached upon a hole in the ground, but toward evening a thunderstorm came up with heavy rain and water ran into the hole and rendered it useless as a dwelling for the bees. On the next day the old scouting bees came, but they no longer campaigned for this nesting place in the cluster. The decision reverted to another nesting place, which, though discovered earlier, had been judged as second class in comparison with the hole in the ground.

A third case was quite similar. One of my artificial bee

cases was reckoned as a dwelling of the first order, and again the scouting bees suddenly stopped dancing shortly before the move. Only a careful examination explained the matter. Through a narrow crack *ants* had entered the box and laid down their pupae in the warm, protected room, and so this nesting place too had become useless as a future bee dwelling.

Thus we may see the deeper biological meaning in delay of the agreement, often for days. In this way a premature decision is avoided and we now understand that strange behavior of the scouting bees in repeatedly returning to the empty nesting place, although there is nothing there to be gathered, like nectar or pollen. Through repeated inspections the scouting bees can assure themselves that the nesting place has not become limited in its excellence even in changed situations and under different weather conditions.

And now back to our actual problem. Besides the location of a dwelling for the bees, the space available and the method of construction of the new home must naturally be taken into consideration. I was repeatedly astounded at how the scouting bees chose the hollows of trees or holes in the ground whose volume corresponded almost exactly to that of our nesting boxes. A mouse hole was indeed inspected, but was recognized immediately as not suitable. A large box in a storage room was likewise discovered by the scouting bees and given a looking over, but here too a single inspection was sufficient, and the site was of no further interest. Though large enough, yet apparently by very reason of its size, it could be warmed only with difficulty. Here it was noteworthy that not every swarm placed the same value on the size of the dwelling; the beekeeper is acquainted with very large swarms, but also with very little ones, the so-called dwarf swarms.

Once we offered such a dwarf swarm, which was scarcely

larger than a man's fist, two dwelling places of the same kind, such as in earlier experiments had been accepted by normal swarms. This time, however, we could entice the swarm into neither of the two boxes. Only when we made one of them smaller by filling up half of the interior space with excelsior was this less roomy compartment agreeable, and the swarm moved in.

As far as the type of construction goes, our experiments indicate the importance of the dwelling's being free of drafts; this is true at least for the climatic region of Bavaria. The wall insulation also appears to be taken into consideration. A hole in the ground is preferred to a wooden building, this latter to a straw basket.

Completely unexpected, however, was the finding that the *distance* of the future dwelling from the mother hive also plays a role. I had noticed that the moving occasionally caused difficulties, particularly when the queen was old and not capable of flying well. In one case she got lost and the swarm had to return to its original home; in three other cases the swarm made a stop during the flight. The queen lay on the ground or in a bush exhausted and after a resting period of several hours the trip was continued. One might then assume that, if distance plays a role, nearby nesting places would be preferred. But exactly the opposite is the case. If two equally good nesting places of varying distances are offered, the one, for example, 30 meters away, the other 300 meters, then the latter is preferred. Finally one recognizes the biological significance: if the swarms move farther away from the mother hive, they will have the possibility of finding new feeding territories at the new dwelling site and not have to share the home feeding grounds with one another. We have not yet established with exactness what distance is optimal for a new dwelling.

∼ Which Bees Function as House Hunters? ∼

In conclusion we shall take up a final problem. House hunting is an occupation that is not provided for in the schedule of a worker bee (see p. 11), and it does not come at any special point of time in the life of the bee. It should be taken into consideration that the "profession" of house hunter does not exist for most bees. Even if a population should send off a swarm every year, half of the bees would remain in the mother hive and not be called to the occupation of house hunting. And in the meantime four, six, or even more generations of worker bees may pass, without there being a need to look for a dwelling. In May, however, when the old queen moves out with the swarm, there must be house hunters, and they must exercise their function skillfully, for the fate of the young population is now dependent on their powers of seeking and on the correctness of their judgment. Where do these scouting bees so suddenly come from? Is there perhaps a special caste of house-hunting bees in the bee colony, which for the entire year have custody over empty dwelling places, gather experience in the establishing of quarters, and await only the time of their call to duty?

In order to obtain an answer to this problem—which involves the very existence of the bee community—the following experiment was set up. In April a feeding place was constructed at a distance of 320 meters from a mother population, at which sugar water was daily provided. The forager bees that visited here were individually marked. When the population set up the first queen cells in May and prepared themselves for swarming, two empty boxes as artificial nesting places were placed at their disposal next to the feeding place. At first there was no interest in these nests.

The bees continued to collect diligently from the feeding dishes (Fig. 25). A few days before the swarming, however, we noticed that the zeal for collecting at the feeding place had diminished and most of the marked bees remained at home. The beekeeper is well acquainted with this behavior

FIG. 25. This feeding table and both empty nesting boxes were offered to a population ready for swarming, which was 320 meters away. Shortly before the moving out of the swarm the former collectors abandoned the feeding table and made inspections of the two nesting boxes. As house-hunting bees they announced these nesting places in the cluster by means of dances.

of a swarming population and he knows that the lazy sitting around of the bees in the hive and at the flight board is the sign for an early moving out of the swarm. The feeding place, however, did not remain completely deserted. Some (perhaps four to six) of the old, marked bees came back occasionally to the feeding table, but no longer as forager bees; they sipped only briefly at the sugar water, but they did not fly back immediately to the hive. Rather they began working in the neighborhood in a strange way: they sought nearby for dark holes and cracks, crawled into mouse holes in the ground and into deep cracks in the bark of trees, and finally inspected the two empty nesting boxes. There was no doubt about it: *these former forager bees had become house-hunting bees.* And it was also these same bees that continued the search for a dwelling after the moving out of the swarm.

There is therefore no special caste of house-hunting bees in the bee community; rather the necessary house hunters are recruited from the forager bees who are familiar with the territory. The really new surprise here was the fact that the seeking of a dwelling by the field bees was not caused first by the moving out of the swarm, but that the seekers of quarters started exercising their function a few days earlier. From this arises still another problem: why did these house hunters give up their hereditary occupation of collecting only a few days before the swarming and not weeks beforehand?

We come here upon a central problem of social regulation and agreement, which will be touched only on the surface: swarming always takes place at a time of abundance, when the blossoms offer their nectar and pollen in large amounts. And, if the beekeeper does not interrupt the natural course of events, then within a short time all the storage chambers in the hive will be filled up. The nest for the brood can therefore not be expanded, the space in the old dwelling place becomes too crowded, and the forager bees are no longer able to give up their food deliveries; they are sentenced to idleness and therefore sit around lazily in the hive. Even before it has progressed so far, the first queen cells have been set up, and now, as the idleness in the hive steadily increases, some of the former forager bees take the initiative: they change over to the only other possible function, and that is house hunting. In this way it is guaranteed not only that the forager bees at the time of swarming cease their restless collecting activities, but also that the search for a dwelling is promptly begun at the very same time. On the other hand, the seeking of quarters and swarming are bound by necessity to good times of collecting. This too has a deeper biological meaning: the young swarm must have the new home set up before the beginning of winter. It must have the new honeycombs finished, it must have taken care of providing offspring, which can then outlive the winter, and it must bring in the necessary provisions for winter. All of this would not be possible if sufficient natural food sources were not available.

3

Developmental Stages
of the Bees' "Language"

THERE IS NO FORM of communiction in the animal kingdom
that is in any way comparable to the dance of the bees.
Through simple symbolic signs, the bees communicate to
each other a factual material rich in content when they announce a good food source or a suitable dwelling place.

We asked ourselves whether our honeybee, *Apis mellifera,*
is really the only animal that has such a highly developed
form of communication. Or does the bees' dance occur also
at least in related species and genera, perhaps only in
modified form and with a different significance? We especially wanted to know which components of the bees' dance
are the "simpler," that is, phylogenetically older, ones, and
whether such primitive stages could be found anywhere
else among the social insects.

∼ Modifications of the
Bees' Dance Within the Genus Apis ∼

Within the species *Apis mellifera* we can already find small geographic modifications of the bees' dance—like a kind of dialect. Von Frisch (1951) has observed that *A. mellifera ligustica*, the Italian bee, has a slower dancing rhythm than *A. mellifera carnica*, the Austrian bee. Baltzer (1952), Tschumi (1950), and Hein (1950) described a new form of dance, the "sickle dance," by means of which the Italian honeybees are able to indicate a direction even within short

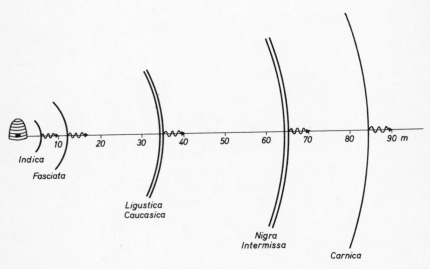

FIG. 26. Racial differences in the transition from round to tail-wagging dance. In each case, goals lying outside a certain radius (indicated by an arc) are described by a directional tail-wagging run. Goals lying within this radius are communicated through nondirectional round dances.

distances from the hive. Boch (1957) extended these comparative investigations to four additional races, the German, Punic, Caucasian, and Egyptian honeybees. He found that the area indicated by a round and by a tail-wagging dance, respectively (Fig. 26), and the dancing rhythm, differ for each of these six races. (Table 1).

TABLE 1. The race specificity of the tail-wagging dance of *Apis mellifera*. The table shows the number of complete cycles of the figure-eight-shaped tail-wagging dance per 15 seconds for each race of bees at several distances from the hive to the source of food. (After Boch 1957.)

RACE	DISTANCE OF THE FEEDING TABLE (METERS)					
	50	100	200	300	400	500
Ligustica Spin.	9.6	9.05	7.3	6.4	5.85	5.2
Carnica Polm.	—	9.8	9.45	7.4	6.75	6.2
Mellifera L.	—	9.25	7.85	6.9	6.0	5.8
Caucasica Gorb.	9.7	8.4	7.3	6.25	5.6	5.15
Intermissa But. Reep.	—	9.0	7.8	7.05	5.9	5.8
Fasciata Latr.	9.2	7.95	6.1	6.25	4.6	4.35

Boch then inquired whether the bees misunderstood each other when he put different races together to make a mixed colony. This is indeed the case. If, for example, an Austrian bee receives information from an Italian bee about a food place 100 meters from the nest, she will fly 120 meters, because she interprets the "Italian dialect" in her Austrian way. And conversely, the Italian bee will fly only 80 meters when given information for 100 meters by an Austrian bee. Similar misunderstandings exist also between other races. It is now clear that each geographic race has its own dialect.

In view of these differences between races, we began to

FIG. 27. A colony of *Apis florea,* the dwarf honeybee, in its natural nest site. A single comb is fastened to a tree branch, and here the colony remains in the open, with all its honey and food reserves, throughout the year.

wonder what "linguistic" differences there might be between full *species* of bees.

In the original home of our honeybee, in India and southeast Asia, there exist three additional species of the genus *Apis: A. indica* Fabr., *A. florea* Fabr., and *A. dorsata* Fabr. Of these, *A. indica* most closely resembles our European honeybee in its behavior; it builds several honeycombs in a hollow tree and it can be kept as a domesticated bee. The more primitive nest structure of *A. florea* and *A. dorsata,* however, shows that they are less closely related; they build only a single honeycomb, in the open air (Figs. 27–30).

All three Indian species announce food sources and nesting sites with round dances and tail-wagging dances

Fig. 28. The bees have been brushed away from the lower part of the comb, to show the brood nest. One can see worker brood, drone brood, and queen cells.

Fig. 29. Several colonies of the giant honeybee, *Apis dorsata,* which have settled together on a "bee tree." Here, also, each colony builds only a single comb and remains in the open throughout the year.

FIG. 30. A colony of giant honey-bees (also called "rock bees") which has settled on a protruding rock.

similar to those of *A. mellifera*. However, the differences already mentioned as racial characteristics within the species *A. mellifera* are now far more pronounced. As Fig. 26 shows, the shift from the round dance to the tail-wagging dance occurs in Austrian bees at 90 yards; the distance becomes shorter and shorter as we go to Italian, Caucasian, and Egyptian bees. Finally, Indian bees are able to indicate a direction through tail-wagging dances from 2 meters onward. With respect to the *rhythm* of the tail-wagging dances, one finds also species-specific codes for distance, again with a transition from *carnica* to *dorsata, ligustica, indica,* and *florea* (Fig. 31).

All these differences in the indication of distance, however, are unimportant; they are so to speak, "dialects" of the bees' language. But when we compare the modes of indicating the direction, we find a peculiarity in one species that gives us some insight into the phylogenetic development of these methods of communication. *A. indica,* the nearest relative of our honeybee, shows no peculiarity in this respect; she dances the same way as *A. mellifera* and reports direction with the same code, in which a tail-wagging run upward means "direction toward the sun," a tail-wagging run downward, "direction opposite the sun," and so forth.

The more primitive dwarf honeybee, *A. florea,* however, whose ancestors never retreated into the darkness of a hollow

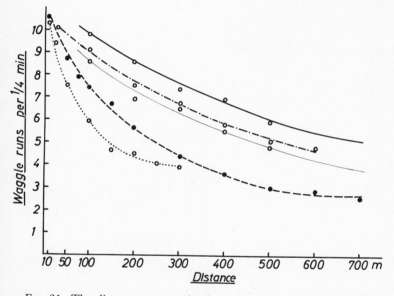

FIG. 31. The distance communication of the three species of Indian bees, as compared with that of *Apis mellifera carnica* (*heavy line*) and *A. mellifera ligustica* (*light line*). The dwarf bee, *A. florea* (*dotted line*) has the slowest dance rhythm, which means that she can indicate nearer goals with more precision. Correspondingly, her scouting area is limited to a radius of 350 meters. *A. indica* (*dashed line*) is next; her flight area extends to about 750 meters. *A. dorsata* (*dot-dash line*) approaches the European bees in her dance rhythm.

FIG. 32. Comb of *Apis florea* from above, showing the widened honey chamber.

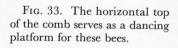

FIG. 33. The horizontal top of the comb serves as a dancing platform for these bees.

tree but remained everywhere children of the sun, do not transpose the solar angle into a vertical direction. It dances only in the open air, on a horizontal surface. When these dwarf honeybees come back from the feeding place, one can see them rush up on the comb, and then they dance on the wide platform on the top of the honeycomb (Figs. 32 and 33); this way, of course, they do not have to transpose the angle between feeding table and sun into terms of gravity, but have only to assume a position with the same angle to the sun as that of the flight to the feeding place, in order to indicate the direction to the goal.

That *A. florea* in dancing really needs a horizontal surface can be shown in the following way:

(1) If one cuts the branch from which the comb hangs, and turns the comb about a horizontal axis so that the originally horizontal dancing platform is now vertical (Fig. 34), then all dancers immediately stop dancing, run up to the new top, try to stamp out a new miniature platform by

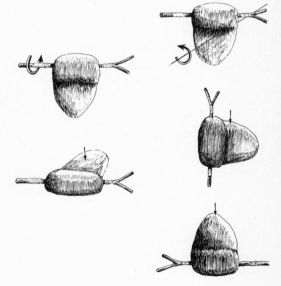

FIG. 34. Rotation experiments, to show that *Apis florea* is able to indicate direction only on a horizontal surface. The circular arrow indicates the direction of rotation; the small arrow points to the dancing surface after rotation.

running about through the mass of bees, and there continue their dance.

(2) If one covers the dancing platform, say with a notebook, then at first the dancers are completely confused; but when after a short time a few bees have assembled on the upper surface of the notebook, the dancers land on the notebook and continue the dance with their old eagerness.

(3) If one deprives the collectors of any possibility of finding a horizontal surface, by placing a roof-shaped piece of glass on top of the comb (Fig. 35), dancing ceases completely. A few bees do try to dance also on the vertical comb surface, but they accomplish only disoriented dances.

A. dorsata, the giant honeybee, appears somewhat intermediate between the European honeybee and the dwarf honeybee. She communicates directional information in a manner between that of *A. florea* on the one hand and *A. mellifera* and *A. indica* on the other. She does dance on the vertical surface; the comb in this case is fastened by its upper edge to a tree branch or wooden beam, and therefore does not offer a horizontal dancing floor. She also transposes properly according to the same code as *indica* and *mellifera;* but it was noticeable that she danced only on those spots of the comb from which she had a free look at the sky. This matter requires further investigation, but it is conceivable that novices following her dance can understand the information more easily when, in the presence of the sun, at the time of the dance itself they can directly see the indicated direction *in natura.*

In summary, we can say that we found in all four species of the genus *Apis,* that is, among the very nearest relatives of our honeybee, essentially the same method of communication—by round dances and tail-wagging dances—as far as food provision and search for housing sites are concerned.

68

Fig. 35. When the top ridge of the comb was covered by a pointed glass roof, the dancers were forced to perform on a vertical surface. As a result, their dances were completely disoriented.

With respect to the distance information that is expressed in the rhythm of the tail-wagging dance, we found only minor differences. In indicating the direction we did find a decisive and more primitive stage in the dance of the dwarf honeybee, but we have to admit that even the more primitive dance of the dwarf honeybee on a horizontal surface still represents a most highly complicated means of communication. Whether we could find something similar and perhaps simpler in another genus was the question for further investigation.

~ Communication Among Stingless Bees ~

The bees most closely related to the genus *Apis* in their social organization are the stingless bees of the subfamily Meliponini (Fig. 36). They use wax as a building material,

FIG. 36. A colony of stingless bees, *Trigona (Cephalotrigona) capitata* F. Smith, in a hollow tree. The brood combs are at the bottom, and above them are the honey and pollen containers, about the size of a hen's egg.

they collect and store nectar and pollen, and colonies are divided by means of swarming just as in *Apis*.

If we now want to study means of communication among the stingless bees, it is important to point out a few peculiarities in their way of life. It will then become clear that Meliponini as a whole are on a lower order of social organization than *Apis*. (The following experiments were carried out in Brazil together with Dr. W. E. Kerr, whose great experience and knowledge of the biology of stingless bees were of decisive assistance to this study.)

The nest structure of many species is cluster-shaped and, even in those cases where we find regular horizontal combs, the cells face in only one direction, opening upward (Figs. 37–39).

In the nursing of the brood, the stingless bees do not know progressive feeding customary with our honeybee. The normal print—a crucial keynote for a high social caste system—is far less completely developed than in our bees. For instance, collecting of nectar and building of comb, or

70

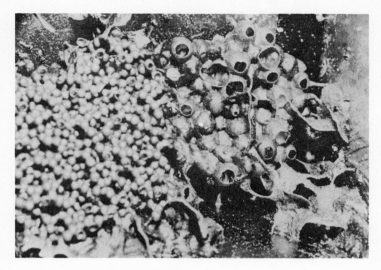

FIG. 37. Nest building in *Trigona iridipennis* F. Smith, a very primitive stingless; bee. Not only the food-storage containers (*right*) but also the brood cells (*left*) are roundish structures built irregularly on top of one another.

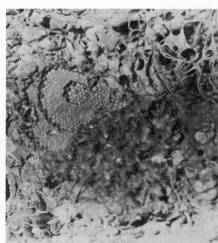

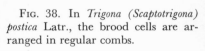

FIG. 38. In *Trigona (Scaptotrigona) postica* Latr., the brood cells are arranged in regular combs.

FIG. 39. Two brood combs of *Trigona (Scaptotrigona) postica* at higher magnification; the combs lie horizontally and are not built in adjacent double layers, as in *Apis,* but consist of a single layer of cells. The opening of the cells points upward.

collecting and concentrating of nectar, can be carried out by one and the same bee at the same time. This means that the specialization in the division of labor has not progressed as far as in *Apis.*

With respect to *mutual communication* among the stingless bees, *all eleven species so far investigated have a means of communication that enables them to alert other bees and guide them to a specific goal.* The method of the Meliponini is, however, different in many points from that of *Apis.* This method, taken as a whole, is more primitive and corresponds to the primitive level of their social development.

First let us observe the success of such an alerting process in the respective species. A feeding place is frequented by five marked bees, and we count the newcomers that assemble within 1 hour. The results are indicated in Fig. 40

72

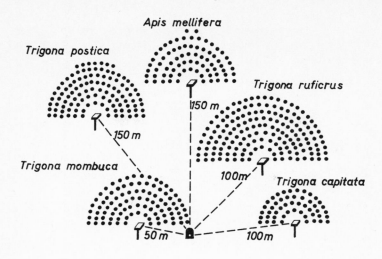

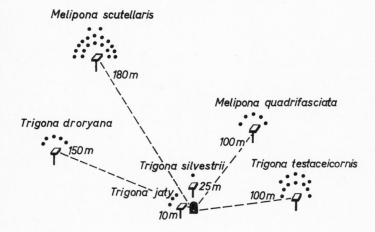

Fig. 40. A comparison of the success of various stingless bees in alerting new foragers. In each experiment, five marked collector bees visited a feeding table. Each black dot represents a newcomer who arrived at the feeding table within 1 hour. Each of these newcomers was caught and put in alcohol, so that it was unable to alert the hive further.

73

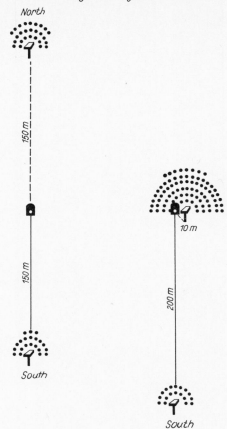

Trigona droryana

FIG. 41. An experiment to test whether direction or distance information can be communicated in stingless bees. In addition to the training table (*solid line* from hive to table), a control table (*broken line*) was set up, in a different direction or at a different distance from the hive. Again the alerted newcomers were caught and counted at both tables. This species—*Trigona (Plebeja) droryana* Friese—shows no indication of any directional or distance communication. Newcomers fly in the opposite direction as well as in the "training" direction, and in the distance experiment the nearby control table receives many more visitors than the "training" table.

74

and compared with those derived from *Apis*. We see that the majority of the species investigated cannot compete with *Apis* in their alerting efficiency. But among them are four species that are able to bring just as many if not more newcomers to the goal within the same time as our honeybee.

We now go one step further and ask: are the alerted novices being informed about the position of the goal? So besides the regular feeding place we put a second one, which is marked with the same scent but stands at a different distance or in a different direction. No collector bees frequent this control table (Figs. 41 and 42). We want to know how many if any newcomers come to this control table, that is to say, whether information has been given about the *direction* to the feeding place or about its *distance*.

The various species show a different behavior in this respect. Those species, such as *Trigona droryana,* which could not compete with the honeybee in their alerting efficiency do not show any communication of directional or distance information. The newcomers visited the control table in the

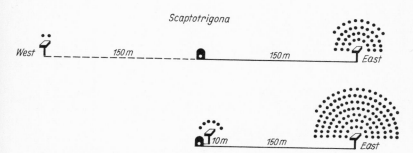

FIG. 42. The same experiment as in Fig. 41. *Trigona (Scaptotrigona) postica* was able to alert newcomers directionally, toward the training table. Almost no newcomers appeared in the opposite direction, and even the nearby control table, only 10 meters away, was hardly noticed.

opposite direction just as frequently as the one in the training direction; and tables standing nearby may even be more often visited than the original feeding place at a greater distance (Fig. 41). The other species with high alerting efficiency, however, were able to send their novices specifically directed to the goal (Fig. 42). Seemingly they had as good a method of indicating direction and distance as *Apis mellifera.*

We found, however, that this is not the case and that these stingless bees do not have a method of directly transmitting information on direction and distance. When we looked into the observation hive we did not see anything that would suggest in any way directed or rhythmic dancing movements. The forager bees did run excitedly around in the hive before and after nectar delivery, and in between made some shaking movements with their body, but one could never see the hive bees running very long after these supposed "dancers." At best they were momentarily attentive; there was no trace of a following of the dancers as in the case of *Apis.* One thing stood out: as soon as the collector bee entered the hive, one could hear a characteristic high-pitched hum, recalling the peeping hum of our queen bee. It sounds like an irregular Morse code signal: $- - \cdot - \cdot - \cdot\cdot$ $- \cdot\cdot\cdot - \cdot - - \cdot$. We were able to prove in specific experiments that this humming had something to do with the alerting reaction.

We divided the beehive into two compartments with a board. Through a sliding door at the entrance hole we could direct the marked collector bees into either one or the other compartment. After a fairly long feeding interval, we allowed a single scout to come to a known feeding place and could now establish that when we allowed her to return into compartment *A* she would also alert her colleagues in compartment *B*. In another experiment we combined two colonies in a single box, separated only by a wire screen. Now we could observe that the humming of a single collector bee of colony *A* would also alert novices of colony *B*. The result of the experiment was negative, however, when we padded the floor with foam rubber. The latter result indicates that the receptor mechanism for these humming sounds is not really hearing, but the vibrational sense. It thus seems to be proved that the humming of the collector bees has an alerting effect. But there were no indications of any communication of direction or distance.

The following observation gave additional information. I noticed that in the case of *Trigona (Scaptotrigona) postica* Latreille—a species with a supposed directional and distance communication—the novices came to the feeding place not alone, but almost always in groups. For example, on 17 December 1956 I trained two marked bees for 150 meters southeast. In 50 collecting flights, between 8:53 and 10:19, they did not bring a single newcomer to the feeding table. But in the following 2 minutes, 57 novices appeared at once. And they arrived simultaneously with the two marked forager bees. Had these novices been piloted to the goal?

To investigate this possibility, we tried to run after the marked bees on their route from the hive to the feeding place and back. But we had no luck, because we quickly lost sight of the little bees in Brazil's luxuriant vegetation. Thereupon we moved the hive to an airport and let the bees fly across the flat landing strip to the feeding place. Here we could, after a little practice, follow them; and what we now saw was indeed remarkable. First the forager bee made three, five, or more normal collecting flights, but thereafter she no longer returned on a straight flight to the

77

hive, but every 2 or 3 yards she settled down on a blade of grass, a pebble, or a clod of dirt, ran about there for 2–3 cm with open mandibles and rubbed them on the substrate, then flew to the next pebble or grass leaf, and so on. Figure 43 shows the record of such an experiment. Very often the bee then did not even return to the hive, but turned around a few meters before the entrance hole and returned a few minutes later, with a group of newcomers, to the feeding place. The most obvious assumption was that odor trail marks were being placed along the flight line and that the alerted novices were guided along this odor trail to their goal.

Obviously, however, these odor trail marks on the ground were alone insufficient to lure the novices, because in that case they would probably have come singly and on their own. Repeatedly we tried to observe whether the novices were following a guide bee, and this we could indeed see under advantageous lighting conditions; sometimes the newcomers followed the guide bee so closely that they caused a collision when the marked bee prepared to alight at the feeding table. Not only that, but we also noticed that after the first collecting flights a fair number of alerted novices would emerge from the entrance hole and assemble in a loose swarm in front of the hive, until they were led away to their goal by the guide bee. This we obtained merely by observation.

We tried to find experimental proof for three assumptions: (1) that the guide bee does indeed place odor trail marks on the ground; (2) that these odor trail marks serve for the orientation of the novices; (3) that the guidance of a leader bee is necessary in addition to the odor trail marks. These experiments were as follows.

(1) If we offered the collector bees prominent landmarks

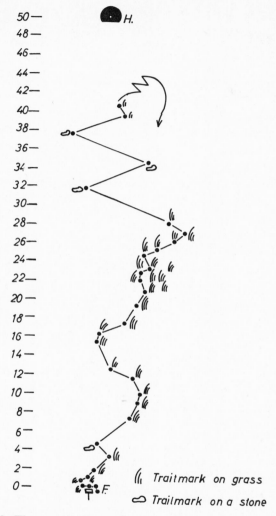

FIG. 43. The record of a trail-marking flight of *Trigona (Scaptotrigona) postica*. Each point indicates one of the short landings on her return flight, during which she deposited an odor trail mark on a blade of grass or a stone. *H,* hive; *F,* feeding table.

on a flat uncultivated area, such as a tall grass blade or a wooden stick thrust in the ground, then the bees landed upon these by preference, and put the odor trailmarks on them. Afterwards we could detect a characteristic odor upon such a grass blade or stick. *This odor was identical with that of the mandibular gland of these bees.* The mandibular gland, therefore, is developed as a scent gland. It consists of a glandular part and a reservoir and opens near the base of the mandibles into a narrow canal (Figs. 44 and 45). Proof thus seems to be offered that the forager bees lay scent trail marks when they alight on the ground, and that the scent secretion comes from the mandibular glands.

(2) In order to test the significance of the scent marks for the orientation of the newcomers, we offered our bees a situation in which they were prevented from leaving scent marks. We placed a hive on the eastern shore of a pond and trained the bees to fly along the northern shore until we reached the feeding table on the western shore. Now the bees always flew across the water, where

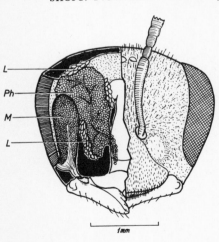

FIG. 44. The head glands of *Trigona (Scaptotrigona) postica;* note the well-developed mandibular glands. *L,* labial glands; *Ph,* pharyngeal glands; *M,* mandibular glands.

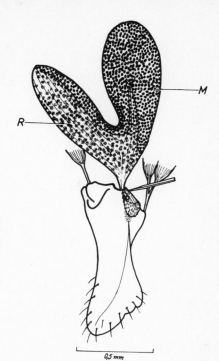

Fig. 45. Isolated mandibular gland of the bee shown in Fig. 44. The gland (*M*) is a hollow structure; the walls are formed by the glandular epithelium, and the inner cavity serves as a reservoir (*R*).

they were of course unable to place any odor marks. They did try it, by flying again and again very low over the water surface. Then they repeatedly returned to the shore, where they generously bestowed scent marks all over the feeding table, and the notebook and hat of the observer.

During the whole feeding time of 2 days, not a single newcomer appeared at the feeding place. Then we strung a rope across the water, and hung a few twigs at 2–3-meter intervals. This now served as a bridge for the newcomers. Within 35 minutes, 37 newcomers reached the goal and we could conclusively observe how the 11 marked collector bees were eagerly placing odor marks on the twigs (Fig. 46).

To test whether the row of twigs over the water might alone have served as an *optical* guiding line over the water, we turned the whole row of twigs 32° to the south, leaving the end near the hive fixed and the feeding place at its old

FIG. 46. As soon as we strung this row of shrubbery across the lake, the new recruits came thronging to the food table. The freshly laid odor marks on the leaves and twigs indicated the trail for them.

spot. The 11 collector bees and the additional 37 novices continued to frequent the feeding place; but now the flow of further newcomers was suddenly interrupted. And there were no new novices at the control table at the end of the row of twigs.

Thus we see that the scent trail marks on the ground are an indispensable aid for the novices in finding the goal, after they have been alerted in the hive.

(3) In order to test whether the odor trail marks *alone* are sufficient to lead newcomers to the goal, we laid out *artificial* trail marks in a false direction, but they did not fool the bees. However, when we placed these artificial marks in the training direction, in addition to the natural odor stations, then the bees noticed them and swarmed vigorously about them.

From this we may conclude that the guidance of a leader

bee is necessary, in addition to the odormarks, to lead the alerted newcomers from the hive to their goal. Further experiments are needed, however, before we can decide whether the leader bees themselves use optical or olfactory clues in flying between hive and goal.

Thus we found a new form of communication in stingless bees. Corresponding to their simpler social organization, it is far more primitive than that of *Apis*. Two characteristic elements of the bees' dance—directional and distance information—are not incorporated in the alerting system of the *Meliponini,* but we do find in this group a few basic elements of the bees' dance. The worker bee returns to the hive and searches for *contact* with other bees by running about excitedly, and *the interested attention of the hive bees is turned toward such a "dancer."* These are also the prerequisites in *Apis* for the alerting and informing of novices by the dancing bees. Furthermore, the *Meliponini* are able to communicate to their companions the important information about *which species of flower has been visited,* when they carry home the scent of that flower in the hairs on their body, together with the nectar, and the novices will search outside for this scent.

The essential difference between the communication of the *Apini* and the *Meliponini* lies in the fact that *Meliponini* newcomers are not directed to their goal by information imparted exclusively within the hive, but are guided in addition by trail marks and pilot bees beyond the hive. *Apis* novices, on the other hand, receive a detailed description of the position of the goal while they are still in the hive, and are thus able to reach the goal independently. It is remarkable that the primitive method of finding the goal with the help of guides can be just as successful as the more elegant method of *Apis*.

There is one point in which the stingless bees are even superior to our *Apis:* if our bees have to report a feeding place much above or below the hive, their method of communication fails (von Frisch, Heran, and Lindauer, 1953). Not so in the *Meliponini.* On 23 March we trained eight bees of *Trigona postica* for the top of a water tower 20 meters high. Within 30 minutes they brought 88 newcomers up to the feeding table. We could observe especially clearly how the marked collectors placed their odor marks on the concrete posts and the iron gate and how thereafter they piloted their followers up. A control experiment with *Apis* at the same place gave negative results, just as it had done earlier on a radio tower in Munich.

Perhaps in the tropical forests of Brazil, with their giant trees, it is advantageous for the *Meliponini* to be able to guide their hive companions upward too, where the crowns of trees are offering their nectar-filled blossoms above the sea of leaves.

Thus we have learned two different forms of communication. The basic elements probably go back to one common root (p. 83), whereas the more special characteristics may have evolved independently.

If we compare the methods of communication of other social insects, we find some common traits among the ants and the stingless bees. Many ant species place odor marks on the route to the feeding place. Novices that have been alerted by excited movements of the foragers follow the odor trail (Brian, 1955; Carthy, 1951; Goetsch, 1953; Holt, 1951; McGregor, 1948; Sudd, 1957, 1959; Wilson, 1959). Thus here we have a combination of alerting and indication of direction.

Surprisingly enough, no similar communication system has thus far been found in foraging bumblebees, although they are so closely related to the honeybee and the stingless bees (Jacobs-Jessen, 1959). Perhaps it is not really too astonishing, because the bumblebee colonies of the temperate zone disintegrate every fall and therefore have no need to collect winter food supplies. For the daily needs no special "language" seems to be necessary. Furthermore, there is no communication necessary about nesting sites, since in our climatic region bumblebees do not swarm. The search for a new home requires an especially effective and highly developed system of communication (Lindauer, 1955, 1958).

On the other hand, in perennial tropical wasp colonies (*Polybia scutellaris* White) I found the existence of a communication system for foraging flights that was similar in effectiveness to that of primitive Meliponini (unpublished). Ten wasps (in Piracicaba, Brazil) brought on the average 5–7 newcomers in 30 minutes to a feeding place 150 meters from the colony. There is no communication of direction or distance. Further experiments on this type of stimulation are planned.

In conclusion, an extremely interesting observation of Dethier (1957) should be mentioned. He describes a curious dancing behavior of the fly *Phormia regina*. If a small drop of sugar solution is offered on a horizontal plane, the fly starts to look for more food after the droplet is eaten. It runs excitedly around with certain characteristic somewhat circular searching movements ("dance"). The movements are disoriented in darkness or diffuse light. However, if a source of light is offered from one side, the runs become oriented parallel to the incident light. If, after stimulation, the plane is shifted from a horizontal to a vertical position and the light is shut off, the paths become oriented with respect to the field of gravity (positive or negative geotaxis).

This quite unexpected observation gives us a hint that

perhaps the excited "dance," performed after finding and tasting a sweet "appetizer," which includes a certain directionality of movements in correlation to the location of the food, might be an innate behavior widely distributed among insects and thus possibly is one of the roots of the elaborate bee dance.

4

Sensory Aspects
of the Bees' Dance

WE HAVE LEARNED THAT THE "LANGUAGE" OF THE BEES'
dance contains a rich store of information. Only because
the bees possess appropriate sensory faculties can they receive and communicate with such precision so many facts
about the position of a source of food as are conveyed
through the tail-wagging dance.

The senses of *smell* and *taste* are employed when the
dancer gives information about the species of flower she has
visited, or when she reports the quality of the food by means
of the vivacity and perseverance of her dancing, according
to a scale that is well understood by the other bees (von
Frisch, 1950).

Particularly excellent sensory performance is demanded
of the bee when she must announce the *location* of the goal.
When she communicates the *distance* of a food source to her
colleagues in the hive, she must first have measured this
distance accurately. On the other hand, the bees who follow
her dance must be able to calculate the distance from the

rhythmic movements that they have perceived in the dark hive; this information then serves for orientation on their flights to the food source.

The demands in the case of *direction* indication are no less complicated: the dancer is able to translate the angle between the direction (that is, the azimuth) of the sun and that of the feeding place into an angle with respect to the force of gravity, as she dances in darkness on the perpendicular comb. This she is able to do with an accuracy of a few degrees. This must mean that she: (1) can sight, with her eyes, the above-defined angle during her flight to the goal with great exactness; and (2) can divide a vertical surface into angular sectors just as exactly with the help of her gravitational sense organs.

Again, the same sensory accomplishments, in reverse order, are demanded of the naive foragers, who must head directly toward the unknown goal after following a dancer through the symbolic dance.

∼ The Determination of Distance ∼

We still do not understand completely how the dancer is able to determine the distance when she is flying from hive to feeding place; but we do have certain important clues.

At first one might guess that the *flying time* serves as a measure of distance for the bee; but that could not be verified. It seems rather to be the amount of *energy* needed during the flight that serves as the basis for distance information. Von Frisch (1948) found that bees indicated a greater distance when they had to fly against a head wind to their food source than when they were flying in a quiet atmosphere. (It is always the flight *toward* the food source that the bees refer to in their dances.) Correspondingly, they reported a shorter distance when they had a tail wind.

Since, moreover, we found that bees actually increase their air speed in a head wind, and decrease it in a tail wind (von Frisch and Lindauer, 1955), the flying time cannot be the indicator for distance measurements.

Heran and Wanke (1952) forced bees to fly uphill to a feeding place. The dancers then reported a longer stretch than they did when flying the same distance downhill (Fig. 47). Again there was correlation of the dancing rhythm with the calculated energy consumption—but not with the flying time.

One can also force the bees to *walk* to a feeding place. In such experiments, a horizontal platform is built on the flight board. On this platform, food is offered at various distances. The whole table is covered with a flat glass roof just 2 centimeters above the platform, so that the bees that are trained to the feeding dishes can reach them only by walking. After walking for about 3 to 4 meters, the foragers will report in their dance a distance corresponding to a *flight* distance of about 100 meters (Bisetzky, 1957). As a foot march of 4 meters takes much longer than a flight of 100 meters, the time itself can again not be a measure of the distance reported.

∼ Communication of Directional Information ∼

As mentioned previously, the accuracy of the directional information depends on how accurately the bee can (1) read the position of the sun, and (2) express an angle with respect to gravity.

(1) Determination of the position of the sun

The choice of the sun as reference point for indicating direction is undoubtedly a good one, for it makes a detailed description of terrain unnecessary. But the sun also has

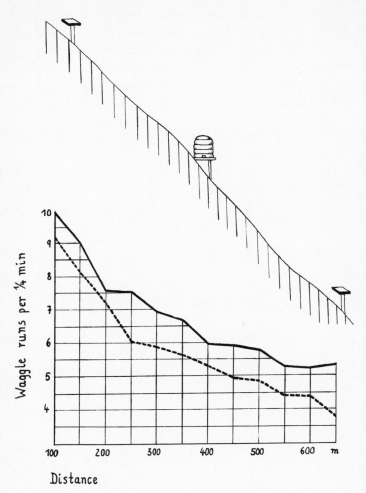

FIG. 47. *Above:* Sketch of the site of the hillside experiment; *below:* distance indication of dancers that had visited the uphill or downhill feeding place. *Solid curve:* number of tail-wagging runs per quarter minute of the downhill collectors: *broken curve:* number of tail-wagging runs of the uphill collectors. The latter indicate a distinctly longer distance, with their slower dancing rhythm, than the downhill collectors.

some peculiarities that one must take into account if one wants to use it as a compass: it disappears from time to time, behind clouds, mountains, or the edge of a forest, and it does not remain in one place but changes its position from morning to evening, and its course from spring to fall. In the Northern Hemisphere it seems to move in a clockwise direction; in the Southern Hemisphere, counterclockwise.

Since it has been shown that the bees still perform oriented dances even under such difficult conditions, the suspicion arose that they perhaps had a substitute reference system in reserve, which could be used to supplement the solar compass when necessary. The following experiments were designed to test this possibility.

One of the most critical situations the bees meet with occurs in the tropics where the sun goes through the zenith twice yearly. At these times, one would expect the dancers to find themselves helpless, because one cannot indicate any direction on earth by using the position of the sun when it stands at the zenith.

I observed a community of bees in Ceylon during the approach of the sun to the zenith; now they would be forced to demonstrate whether they could adapt to such a situation at all, and whether they perhaps had a second compass, in addition to the sun, to indicate direction. As the sun approached nearer and nearer to the zenith, the collector bees—to my surprise— suddenly began to stay at home. This was no doubt the most comfortable solution for them, in order to avoid an embarrassing situation. I had to use a trick to lure them to the feeding place at noon. From early morning on, every half hour, we presented small samples of sugar solution at the feeding place; from 11:30 to 12:30, however, a full meal was offered. This stimulated collecting ambitions so greatly that the bees now collected

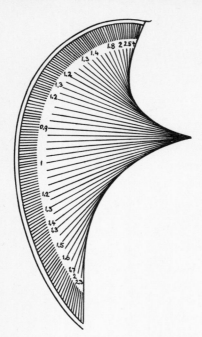

FIG. 48. Sagittal section through the bee eye, indicating the angle (degrees) between the axis of individual ommatidia in various regions of the compound eye. The angle of divergence of the ommatidia that face upward (about 3°) agrees well with the accuracy of measurement of the solar azimuth that is exhibited by the bees when the sun passes through the zenith. (After Baumgärtner, 1929).

even during the critical hours. And now the bees had to lay their cards on the table: in the hive, they now produced completely disoriented dances, whether the comb was vertical in darkness or horizontal in sunlight, thus showing that the sun was their only compass.

That experiment yielded at the same time information about our first question: *how accurately can bees read the azimuth of the sun?* The disoriented dances started only 10 minutes before zenith, and lasted only until 10 minutes after zenith. Thus the bee's eye is able to determine direction with relation to the solar position when the sun is only about 3° off the zenith. By the same token, the bees were able to indicate direction when the sun was passing through the meridian, provided it passed more than 2.5° south or north of the zenith.

Baumgärtner (1929) and Del Portillo (1936) determined many years ago the angle of divergence of the bee's ommatidia and found that it is 2–3° for the apical ommatidia (Fig. 48). This agrees surprisingly well with the results of our observations. The bee's eye is thus and excellent astronomical angle-measuring device.

The sun is, without doubt, the only compass that the dancers use for indication of direction. It is astonishing how well they are able to overcome the other handicaps previously mentioned, which are inherent in the use of a sun compass for orientation.

Determination of the sun's position when it is behind clouds. When von Frisch lectured in the United States 10 years ago about the language of the bees, he had just discovered that the tiniest patch of blue sky suffices to reveal the sun's position to the bees—even though the sun itself may be hidden behind clouds or behind a mountain. The bees are able to recognize the direction of vibration of the polarized light that comes to earth through this clear patch of sky. Since the direction of vibration, together with the percentage of the light that is polarized, determines the sun's position in the sky, the bees are able to reckon the sun's location on the basis of information received from the blue sky (von Frisch, 1950).

Since that time it has been found that the bees are able to locate the sun even on a fully overcast day. They are able to see the sun directly through the clouds (provided they are not too thick), even when it is not visible to our eyes. This ability depends on the fact that 5 percent more ultraviolet light penetrates through the clouds directly in front of the sun than elsewhere in the sky, and this difference is enough for the bee eye to be able to distinguish the sun from the surrounding sky. From other experiments it is well known that bees are particularly sensitive to ultraviolet light (von Frisch, Lindauer, and Schmeidler, 1960).

Compensation for detours or deviations due to side winds. The bees do not always fly in a straight line to the feeding place, but in an irregular curved line. Frequently a side wind will force them to assume a flying position headed at an angle into the wind, in order to compensate for the drift. They will then view the sun from another angle during the whole flight than that assumed for a perfectly straight flight between hive and goal (Fig. 49). To our surprise, we found that in this case also the dancers in the hive indicate the angle to the sun according to a hypothetical direct-line

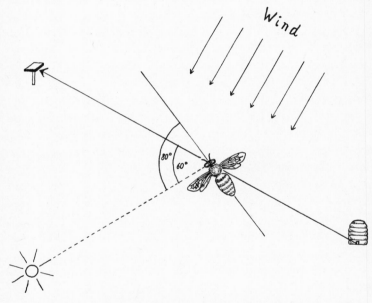

FIG. 49. The bee compensates for drift in a side wind by flying obliquely into the wind. This means, however, that she sees the sun at a different angle (here 80°) from the actual angle between sun and feeding place (60°). But even in this case, the forager bee indicates in dancing the angle corresponding to a theoretical direct flight between hive and feeding place.

flight. This means that they had to correct for the deviation due to their actual oblique flying position (von Frisch and Lindauer, 1955). Also when the bees were forced to make detours around a forest, a house, or a rock, in dancing they always reported only the straight-flight direction, which they actually never flew. Therefore in the case of side winds and in detour experiments, some kind of central calculating mechanism must inform the bee of the angle of drift.

Compensation for the sun's motion. The sun can be used as reference point for orientation only when one takes account of its progress along its regular, predetermined path. The same holds true for the indication of direction by the tail-wagging dance. Someone may object that this apparent movement of the sun is so slow that the dancers normally do not have to worry about it, as the dance follows immediately after the collecting flight, so that the position of the sun is practically the same during the flight and during the dance. Under certain conditions, however (Lindauer, 1957), there are "marathon dances" in the hive; a bee will then dance in the dark hive not for 1 or 2 minutes, but for hours without collecting flights in between. Such a marathon dance may even continue into the night. In the meantime, of course, the solar position changes considerably. And in fact the dancer changes her directional information according to the movement of the sun (Fig. 50), without ever observing the solar position directly through the entrance hole.

This can be explained only if the bee has the faculty of compensating for the movement of the sun. For that an inner "clock" mechanism is needed. This means an accurate time sense and an excellent ability to correlate time and solar position. I shall describe in more detail in the next

95

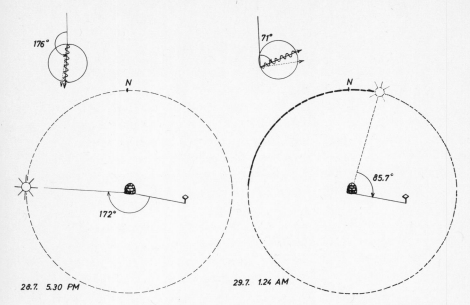

Fig. 50. Directional indication in a "marathon dance'" The bee was fed at 5:30 in the evening, before sunset, at a feeding place in the east. She saw the sun at an angle of 172° to the right of the feeding table. In dancing (*upper left*) she made an error of 4°. After midnight (1:24 a.m.), she was incited to dance in the hive. In dancing, she again referred to the sun in indicating direction. Although she could never have seen the sun's position at this time of night, she made an error of only 14° in calculating its supposed angle (85.7°) with respect to the feeding place.

chapter this ability of the bees to calculate solar movement, and some problems of orientation connected with it.

(2) The gravitational sense organs of the bee and their performance in directional information

We shall now leave the subject of vision for the present, and turn to the darkened hive, where all the optical impressions that the foragers have gathered outside must be transposed into terms of the direction of gravity.

Up to now, very little has been known about the sense of gravity in insects. Receptors are known only in water bugs and water beetles, located on the abdomen or at the bases

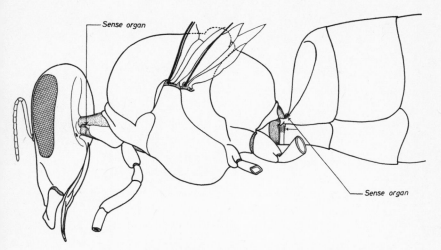

FIG. 51. Location of the static sensory organs on the neck articulation and petiolus (articulation between thorax and abdomen). The head has been forced forward, out of the articulation, to make visible the chitin cones with sensory bristles on the episternum.

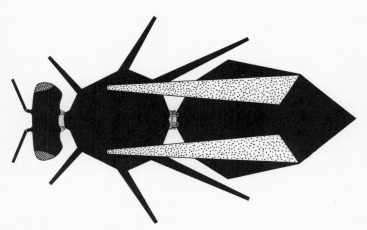

FIG. 52. Location of the sensory organs, dorsal view (schematic).

of the antennae; these receptors are capable of detecting the upward pressure of an air bubble (Baunacke, 1912; Rabe, 1953; Weber, 1933). In bees, we found (Lindauer and Nedel, 1959) tufts of sensory elements at the joints between head and thorax, and between thorax and abdomen, which serve as receptors for gravity (Figs. 51 and 52).

The sense organ on the head-thorax articulation. The head is suspended loosely on two chitinous pegs or protrusions of the episternum, which extend into the occipital region of the head. These pegs have rows of sensory hairs on their outer surface. The sensory hairs are evenly in contact with the head capsule when the head is in a normal position, that is, when the bee is standing on a horizontal surface. To the right and left of the occipital hole, the head has semicircular, smoothly polished ridges of chitin in corresponding positions. The chitin pegs are hollow, and the cavities have a median slit through which, on each side, a nerve leads from the first thoracic ganglion to the sensory tufts and connects there with about 180 bipolar sensory cells. We call this the *nervus cervicalis* (Figs. 53–55).

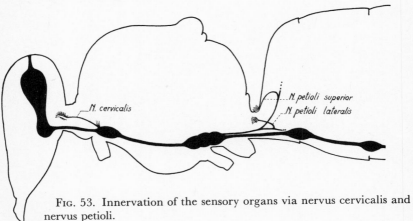

FIG. 53. Innervation of the sensory organs via nervus cervicalis and nervus petioli.

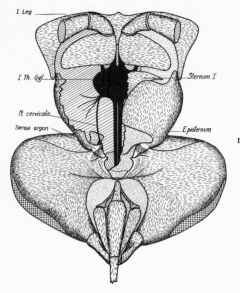

FIG. 54. Ventral view of the neck organ, with its innervation.

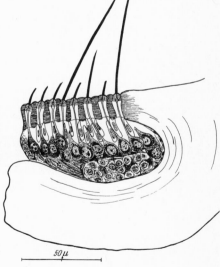

FIG. 55. Cross section through the episternal cone, showing the sensilla trichodea of the stato-organ.

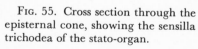

Mittelstaedt (1950) has described similar anatomic arrangements in the head articulation of the dragonflies. In this case, however, they are regarded not as static organs, but as "dynamic" organs which respond to acceleration. Together with the dorsal light response, they make possible maintenance of equilibrium in flight, by detection of rapid movements of the head relative to the thorax.

In bees, the function of this sensory organ as a stato-receptor can be interpreted—at first theoretically—in the following way. The head can be rotated about a transverse axis, pivoting on the double joint formed where the head rests on the two chitin pegs; the apex of the forehead then moves forward or backward. A passive rotation around the longitudinal axis (moving the right or the left eye upward) is possible within only a small range. A free rotation around the longitudinal axis is possible by a rotation together with the episternal plates of the prothorax. The center of gravity of the head is ventral to this joint; the weights of the upper and lower head parts are approximately 2.5 and 6.5 mg, respectively. When the bee crawls from a horizontal surface onto a vertical comb, the head will fall toward the sternum, or when the bee runs downward it will fall toward the back, since each time the heavy ventral half of the head will tend downward like a pendulum.

This effect can be demonstrated with a freshly killed bee from which the muscles of the neck, as well as the ventral nerve cord and the pharynx, have been excised at the neck, so that the head hangs only by two tendons on the chitin pegs. In the horizontal position, the head capsule has almost equal contact with the hairs of the two sensory tufts. As the bee assumes a more vertical position, the head pivots on its transverse axis, and both sensory tufts will be subjected to a shearing motion. As the longitudinal axis of the bee becomes more steeply inclined, different areas of the tufts will be stimulated maximally, simultaneously, and equally on both sides. The situation is different when the bee clings to a vertical surface and rotates about its dorso-ventral axis, that is, when it changes from head-up to head-down position, or vice versa. Now the sensory tufts will be affected by shearing of different intensity on the two sides. Let us assume that the bee is sitting with her head upward, and turns to the left until the head points downward (Fig. 56). The following sequence of stimuli will then occur:

(i) Starting position: maximal shearing stimulus on the hairs of the ventral sensory tufts, equal on both sides;

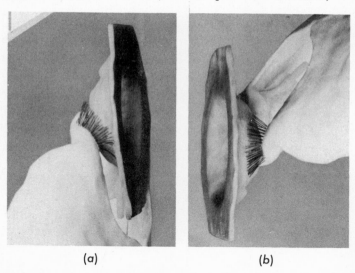

(a)   (b)

FIG. 56. A wax model, to show the shearing action of the head upon the sensory bristles of the neck organ. (a) Let the bee run upward on a vertical wall and the lower bristle area is bent maximally. (b) Let the bee run downward and now the maximal shearing action is transferred to the dorsal bristle region.

101

(ii) Turn counterclockwise until crosswise: the shearing pressure on the right side decreases toward 0; the weight of the head will increasingly press on the left sensory tuft, shifting from the ventral area gradually over the whole sensory field until in the transverse position the weight of the head will press evenly on all the hairs of the left sensory field;

(iii) When the bee now turns farther from the transverse position toward the head-down position, the shearing action on the left sensory tuft will increase, spread toward the dorsal area, and at the same time again engage the right sensory tuft. In the "head-down" position, the maximum shearing pressure will be distributed evenly over the dorsal areas of both sensory tufts.

Specific information corresponding to each position angle should thus be available to the central nervous system, provided the proper central synapses exist. This applies to pivoting about the transverse axis (from a horizontal into an erect vertical position) as well as to pivoting on a vertical surface about the dorsoventral axis. Thus there exists the possibility for a very fine analysis of the position angle on the vertical plane; the degree of bending of individual sensory hairs, and the spatial distribution of the maximal bending within the sensory field, together could provide the necessary information.

We tried to verify this concept experimentally in the following ways.

(1) *Severing the nerves of the sensory organ.* Under certain conditions in a dark room, the bees show a negative geotaxis: they will always run upward. One can insure that all the bees in an experimental group will act this way by the following procedure: if bees in a dark room, on a horizontal surface, are shown a point light source, certain bees will

react with significant positive phototaxis. After the light has been turned off, these same bees will, on a vertical surface, react with clear negative geotaxis.

At this point I would like to make an additional comment: the coupling of these two primitive means of orientation, a positive phototaxis with a negative geotaxis, was in all probability the starting point for transposition of the direction toward the sun into a direction with respect to gravity in the tail-wagging dance. When the food source lies in the same direction (that is, has the same azimuth) as the sun, the positive phototaxis and the negative geotaxis are equal in magnitude and balance each other exactly. The forager flies toward the brightest light in view (the sun) as in a simple phototaxis; and when she later, in the dark hive, transposes the flight direction into a direction with respect to gravity, she heads *upward*, in the tail-wagging dance, with what we can call negative geotaxis. After directional indication has once been established by this relation, we can imagine how other flight directions, deviating to left or right from the direct path with the sun's azimuth, can be transposed on the vertical plane into a direction with respect to gravity.

This translation of a photomenotactic direction into a geomenotactic direction is not an exclusive prerogative of bees. Vowles (1951, 1954) found that ants (*Myrmica ruginodis* Nyl.) run away in a straight line when they are disturbed. On a horizontal plane, the direction of the flight is menotactically oriented toward a source of light. If during flight the plane is shifted into a vertical position and the light is shut off, the ant continues to run straight. But now it maintains the same angle with the direction of gravity as it did before with the light. With equal frequency one of four possibilities is chosen: positive or negative geotaxis, right or left of the perpendicular axis. For instance, a horizontal course 40° to the left of the light may be translated in four different ways on the vertical plane: upward or downward 40° to the left or to the right of the perpendicular. In the dungbeetle (*Geotrupes silvaticus* Panz.) Birukow (1953, 1954) found principally the same conversion key as the bees use when they translate a photomenotactic response into a geotactic response. However, the beetle converts positive phototaxis to positive geotaxis, whereas bees convert it to negative geotaxis.

The transposition of photomenotactic orientation into gravity-dependent orientation is apparently a basic ability of most insects. While this ability may be without special significance in most insects, it has been successfully employed in the communication system of the honeybee, assisting the indication of direction in the tail-wagging dance.

In the following exclusion experiments, the positive phototaxis and the negative geotaxis in the dark hive were used as tests. We denervated the neck sensory organs by severing the nervus cervicalis on both sides right under the chitin pegs, the bees being under carbon dioxide narcosis. They were now, without exception, disoriented when walking on a vertical surface (Fig. 57). Control operations, simple cuts into the skin of the neck, did not diminish their ability to orient themselves correctly. Unilateral severing of the nerve was completely compensated by the bee after a few hours or days; that is, the bees were disoriented at first, but would later show the original negative geotaxis.

We also carried out this severing of the nerve on foraging bees that frequented our artificial feeding place. We intended to observe their dances in the dark hive after the operation. The bees flew back and forth between the hive and the feeding place for days; thus it appears that the sensory organ on the neck is not essential for static orientation during flight. Probably it can be completely replaced in its function by the dorsal light response (experiments concerning this question still need to be done). The experimental bees could not, however, carry out any oriented dances in the hive, provided the two nerves were really severed by the operation. They did show intentions of dancing; sometimes they even attempted a tail-wagging dance, but they never completed one. And the direction of the attempted dances had no relation whatever to the direction of the feeding place.

Occasionally we did notice, however, that such bilaterally denervated bees would start to carry out oriented dances again after a few days. In each case we captured the bees involved and carefully dissected them. It turned out that in all such bees at least one nerve strand was still intact.

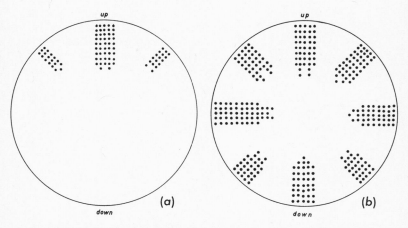

FIG. 57. Experimental proof of the function of the neck organs as gravitational organs. (a) Normal bees run upward on a vertical wall, showing negative geotaxis, when placed in the dark. Each point indicates the direction of one run. (b) In ten bees, the nervus cervicalis was severed on both sides. These bees were disoriented on the vertical wall.

105

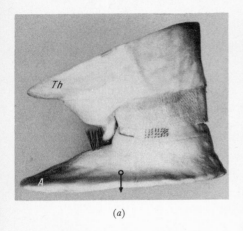

(a)

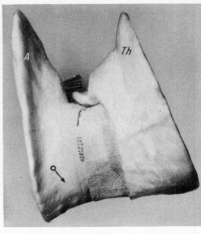

(b)

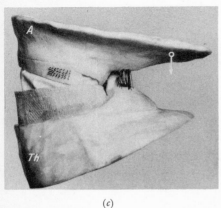

(c)

FIG. 58. Model of the petiolar articulation, with the sensory areas; *A,* abdomen; *Th,* thorax. (*a*) The bee runs upward; the weight of the abdomen pulls downward leaving all sensory bristles free. (*b*) The bee runs on a horizontal plane; the abdomen presses downward, and pushes both lateral sensory bristles partially under the dermal petiolar fold. (*c*) The bee runs downward; the abdomen presses both dorsal sensory bristles against the thorax, leaving both lateral bristle fields free.

The sensory organ is very small and the nerves are difficult to reach, so that failures in the operation cannot always be avoided. From the behavior of the bee we could always predict, however, whether the operation had been successful or not.

(2) *Artificially shifting the center of gravity of the head.* One can artificially shift the center of gravity of the head into the dorsal portion by gluing a piece of lead (10–50 mg) on the apex. Now the apex of the head is the heavy part of the pendulum. And in fact the bee will now confuse "up" and

"down"; in darkness she shows *positive* geotaxis on a vertical surface.

(3) *Immobilizing the head.* We immobilized the head by gluing it to the thorax with a mixture of rosin and wax. Then we also obtained disoriented running on the vertical surface. When the head was then freed again, in the same bees, orientation was as good as before treatment.

But there were exceptions to this. When we succeeded in fixing the head exactly in its normal position the bees still showed negative geotaxis, although somewhat uncertainly. By this experiment, however, the pendulum effect was excluded.

In the same way, we could also find exceptions in experiment (2), when we caused an imbalance by attaching a small piece of lead to the head. If the attached weight was less than 15 mg, the bees still often showed a negatively geotactic run. An uncertainty could, however, be recognized. But from these exceptions in experiments (2) and (3) we concluded that a second sensory organ for gravitational perception must exist.

The sensory tufts on the abdominal articulation. At the point where abdomen and thorax are joined, there are two bilateral pairs of sensory tufts. They are smaller than the neck organ, but are equipped with the same type of sensory hairs and bipolar sensory cells. The shearing on the sensory hairs occurs in this case when the abdomen is bent sideways, the sensory hairs then being pushed under a stiff fold of the abdominal stalk (Fig. 58). A similar shearing action occurs when the bee runs on a vertical surface in a horizontal direction, that is, 90° to the left or right, of vertical. A second pair of sensory tufts lies medially on the abdominal stalk; the weight of the abdomen, in the head-down position, presses the sensory hairs against a corresponding chitin cupola on the thorax. These two pairs of sensory tufts are innervated by the second thoracic ganglion. We call their sensory nerve bundles *nervus petioli lateralis* and *nervus petioli superior* (Fig. 59).

As we have already seen, this second group of stato-receptors can take the place of the neck organ in emergencies. Normally it merely confirms the information supplied by the neck organs, and complements it (especially in the crosswise position referred to previously). We conclude this

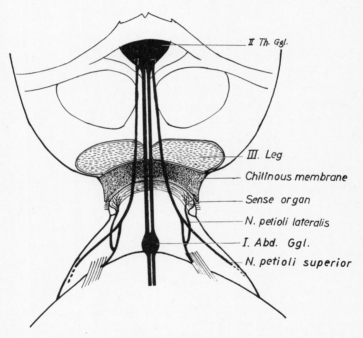

FIG. 59. Innervation of the lateral sensory organs on the petiolus. The nervus petioli superior has been severed; it would run further upward—toward the viewer—to the paired dorsal sensory organs.

from the following observations. When the center of gravity of the head has been shifted, or the head has been glued into a crooked position, the information supplied by the neck organ is wrong. Then the abdominal organ cannot by itself supply the impulses for a negative geotaxis. For this organ to function properly, it is necessary in addition that the neck organ report to the central nervous system: "Head properly oriented"—as is the case when the head is immobilized in the normal position.

If the neck sensory organ is destroyed or if its sensory nerve is severed, the abdominal organ alone is unable to provide static orientation. If the abdomen is glued to the thorax in a normal position but the neck organ is left intact, the negative geotaxis remains unimpaired. Immobilization of the abdomen in a crooked position, however, produces disorientation. Immobilization of both head and abdomen, even in a normal position, destroys static orientation.

There still remain many problems about the sense of gravity that need to be solved. We must investigate in detail, for instance, how these statoreceptors provide information so exact that the dancers are able to indicate an angle with respect to the direction of gravity accurate within a few degrees. One might imagine that, within the strip of sensory hairs lying in a crescent around the chitin pegs, specific rows of these hairs might report to the central nervous system particular vertical angles of orientation of the parts of the body. And the degree and direction of bending of the sensory hairs might also be correlated with the positional angle of the bee's body, as mentioned before. One must keep in mind that the muscles may also play a role in static orientation, as they must constantly keep the head in a normal position, and thus are under differing degrees of tension. This tension could be reported by muscle-stretch receptors. The role of the statoreceptors in free flight also remains to be investigated.

~ Conclusion ~

Probably no means of communication and no act of orientation exists in the entire animal kingdom that requires for success such a constellation of varied sensory perform-ances as the "language" of the bees. And it is not only the correlation in the central nervous system, translating im-pressions from the optical sense into the gravitational sense, or translating a rhythmic tactile sensation into the measure-ment of flight energy and therefore into the estimation of distance, that amazes us; it is also the precision of the purely physiological performance of the sensory organs.

To summarize again:

(1) The olfactory sense serves for the communication of scent information. The dance followers examine the abdo-men of the dancer with their antennae and thus find out which species of flower the collector has visited. The specific scent of the flower clings to the abdominal hairs of the forager, and further scent samples are delivered to the nov-ices through small droplets of nectar.

(2) The sense of taste is used to check the quality of the harvest and determine whether it has the chemical compo-sition that is urgently needed by the colony. Only if it is worth while will the forager dance to recruit novices for as-sistance in collecting.

(3) The eye, the gravitational sense organs, and the time sense are jointly utilized for announcing the direction toward the goal. On the flight to the food source, the angle between the direction of the sun and that of the food source is de-

termined optically. The foragers must remember it until the dance, and then transpose it, with high precision, into an angle with respect to gravity. Not only that, but they must also consider the time interval between the flight toward the goal and the dance, and must compensate for the change in the solar position during this time.

(4) Unsolved questions still remain concerning the sensory performance for *distance* indication. So the field is still open for new discoveries and experiments.

5

Special Problems Concerning Solar Orientation in Relation to the Bees' Dance

IN THE LAST CHAPTER WE MET with some of the problems involved in solar orientation. During recent years we have investigated these problems further, and in this final chapter I should like to report on these experiments separately.

If the bees used the sun as a reference point for their directional indication in dancing, their flights toward the goal must first have been oriented with respect to the sun. Some experiments conducted years ago by Wolf (1926, 1927) gave some hints that this may be the case. The bees were trained to find a feeding table 150 meters north of the hive, and after a while this feeding table, together with the bees sitting on it, was carried to a new location a few meters south of the hive. When the bees were now released from the feeding table, they did not return directly to the hive, but first flew 150 meters southward, as they were used to doing in their normal return flight, and there searched eagerly for the hive (Fig. 60). Only after long searching

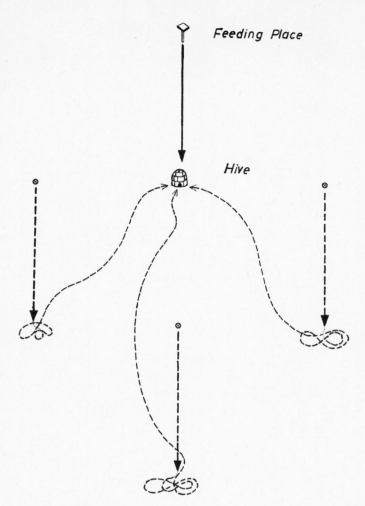

Feeding Place

Hive

FIG. 60. A group of collector bees was captured upon the feeding table they were visiting, the table and bees together were displaced to a point on another side of the hive, and the bees were released. Now they did not fly directly back to the hive, but at first flew in the accustomed southerly direction, and after 150 meters began an obstinate search for the hive. An extraterrestrial fixation point—not landmarks of the surrounding terrain—must have served for their orientation in determining the direction for the home flight. (After Wolf, 1927.)

113

flights did they find their way back to the hive, which was still standing in its original location. They responded in an analogous way when the table was moved to a point west or east of the hive. This means that these bees had oriented themselves on their home flight according to some distant reference point, probably one in the sky.

We can demonstrate this orientation with respect to the sky still more strikingly in the following experiment. A bee colony is transferred to an unknown territory, and a group of collector bees, individually marked with spots of color, is fed at a point about 180 meters south of the hive. This is repeated for several days; the bees learn that there is food to be had *south of the hive*. Overnight, the colony is then displaced into a new, also unknown territory. There, four feeding tables are installed for the bees to choose from: 180 meters to the south, west, north, and east. Each bee that now arrives at one of the tables is promptly captured by an observer, so that it is unable to inform and alert others in the hive. This means that each collector bee must start her flight on her own initiative, choosing her own direction, to search for a food source. No familiar landmark points the direction in which they were formerly trained; only the dome of the sky, crowned by the sun, stands unaltered above the experimental terrain. The trained group of collectors do find their way, unambiguously, to the table in the south. Only the sun can be their guide (von Frisch and Lindauer, 1954).

It still remained to be discovered, however, *how* the bees used their solar compass. Did they keep in mind on each flight, on every training day, which point of the sky was occupied by the sun? And did they—after transposition— memorize the angle between sun and feeding table for each time of the day? Their perfect time sense would enable them to do so (Beling, 1929; Renner, 1957). Or are they even able to compute the movement of the sun for purposes of their solar orientation? The marathon dancers, which we mentioned on page 95, convinced us that this latter ability exists. Our experiment of displacing the hive, in a modified form, was made to furnish new evidence for this fact.

Again a hive was placed in unknown territory, but this time the group of collectors was fed south of the hive only on *one afternoon*. During the succeeding night, the colony was again transferred into strange territory: and now the trained bees must make their choice of direction the next *morning*. The flight hole was opened at 7 a.m., and four feeding tables were placed at the four points of the compass. We counted only those feeding-table visitors that arrived before noon. Had the bees remembered the absolute angle between the sun and the direction to the feeding place, one would expect them to fly in the wrong direction —in this case eastward, since on the preceding afternoon the feeding table had stood to the left of the sun, and now in the morning the feeding table in the *east* occupied the same position with reference to the sun. But again, the collector bees unanimously flew south, thus furnishing additional proof that they can somehow compensate for the movement of the sun, by computation (von Frisch and Lindauer, 1954).

We may now ask the question: how would the bees react when presented with a sun whose position in the sky has been shifted, so that it indicates the wrong direction?

During a stay in Ceylon, I trained the bees to feed at noon at a station 150 meters to the north. This was done in April, when the sun was moving northward, and the training was limited to a few minutes at noontime, when the sun stood exactly in the north, that is to say, in the direction of the feeding place. After a week of training in this way, I took the bees overnight by plane to Poona, India. Poona is just far enough to the north that the noonday sun at the end of April stood exactly as far to the south of the zenith as in Ceylon it was to the north (Fig. 61). Shortly before noon, I opened the flight entrance; four feeding tables were available again, at north, east, south, and west. The bees now flew to the south instead of to the north; in other words, they oriented themselves according to the sun alone, and, since it had been shifted, the bees necessarily mistook south for north (Lindauer, 1957). Thus they demonstrated that the sun was their only compass and that they can use it correctly only in that part of the world where they have been born.

A new question immediately arises, however: is this ability of the bees to orient themselves according to the sun *innate,* or must the bees *learn* the solar orientation appropriate to their geographic location? One might suppose, furthermore, that the bees become *imprinted,* during their preliminary exercise flights (the *"Vorspiel"*), with the direction of movement of the sun and its angular velocity across the sky.

To make the problem clear, we should emphasize to start with that bees live in both Northern and Southern Hemispheres, therefore populations living in different hemispheres must compute for solar movement in opposite directions: in the north, clockwise, and in the south, counterclockwise. In addition, the course of the sun changes with the seasons. An especially complicated situation exists for the bees who live between the Tropics of Capricorn and Cancer; here, during the course of the year, the sun changes twice not only its altitude and its azimuthal angular velocity, but also its apparent direction of movement. Part of the time

116

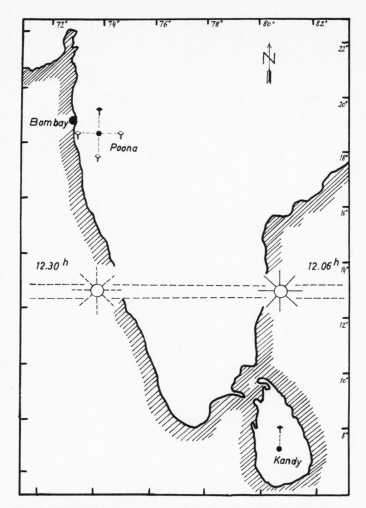

FIG. 61. In Ceylon, bees were trained for a week to feed in the north just as the sun was crossing the meridian (April 16–23). During this time, the sun was north of the zenith, as seen from Ceylon. During the night of April 23–24, the bees were flown by air freight to Poona, India, and released on the next day as the sun crossed the meridian. Now they searched for food in the *south*. This means they had mistaken south for north, because the sun appeared correspondingly displaced in the sky.

117

it seems to move clockwise, then later counterclockwise, as seen from a constant observation point.

To learn whether bees can adapt themselves to a changed and unfamiliar solar movement, we displaced a community by some 40° of latitude. On my return trip from Ceylon to Munich in June 1955, I took with me a colony of Indian bees. At this time of the year in Ceylon the sun moves across the sky north of the zenith. In Munich I trained these Indian bees in the usual way, in the afternoon only, to fly to a feeding place 200 meters to the south of the hive. The bees obviously noticed that something was wrong because the sun was moving through the heavens in the opposite direction from usual: the next morning they were completely disoriented; they could no longer find the southerly direction. Four days later I repeated the training procedure, with the same result.

Only after a stay of *43 days* in their new country were the displaced bees able to relearn the directions. Now the bees trained to a feeding table in the south flew—after transposition—accurately to the south. Thus they proved that they were capable of taking account of the fact that the path of the sun was clockwise in Munich, directly opposite to its counterclockwise course in Ceylon.

It would be of great interest to know whether the bees that "calculated" correctly after 43 days were newly hatched individuals, or workers that had had flying experience before the experimental transplantation. Unfortunately, all collector bees that had been marked in Ceylon died during these 7 weeks; therefore this question remains open. But at least the descendants of the imported queen adjusted to the reversed direction of the sun's movement.

Some time later Kalmus (1956) performed similar experiments. He had a queen bee from North America shipped

118

to Brazil. The offspring, which grew up in Brazil, were subjected to the previously described displacement experiment of von Frisch. According to Kalmus, these North American bees oriented themselves in the Southern Hemisphere approximately as their ancestors had done in the Northern Hemisphere. In other words, they took the sun's course in the south to be clockwise instead of vice versa. It was concluded that this inborn calculating mechanism must be inherited through many generations; only in the course of several centuries would a change-over be possible, based on mutations in the sexual adults (Kalmus, 1956, pp. 563–564).

This conclusion would present a dilemma, at least for those bees whose homes lie between the tropics. As already mentioned, the sun, as seen from a fixed observation point on the earth, changes the direction of its path twice a year in these areas. The bees would therefore have to have two kinds of inborn calculating mechanisms, and accurate knowledge of when to switch from one mechanism to the other would also have to be inherited. Since the life span of a bee is only 4–6 weeks, different generations should inherit different calculating mechanisms.

During my stay in Brazil, I took the opportunity to repeat the experiments of Kalmus, in the same place, and with bees likewise transported from the Northern to the Southern Hemisphere. Despite painstaking care I was unable to confirm the results of his experiments. Apparently some technical differences in the experiments caused the discrepancy in the results.

When we investigate the orientation of the bees by solar compass, through displacement experiments, we take care—after long years of experience—to observe the following precautions:

(1) The colony that is to be used for the experiment must be closed and placed in a cellar during the night preceding the experiment. This is the only way to ensure that all collector bees—the only bees that could accumulate enough experience in solar orientation—are included in the experiment.

(2) On the training day, the colony is not moved into the training area before noon; then, however, one starts immediately with the directional training. In this way one avoids distracting the collector bees, through other food sources, before training starts.

(3) The experimental colony must be so far removed from their original home territory that the new location is situated at least twice the flight radius of collector bees ($\approx$6 kilometers) from the old location. It is known (Wolf, 1926, 1927; Uchida and Kuwabara, 1951) that displaced bees return to their old home as soon as they enter familar territory on their searching flights.

(4) Each collector bee should be individually marked with numbers; and we demand that each numbered bee frequent the feeding table for at least 3 hours without pause. It appears that this is the only way we can be certain that the bees are well trained, that is, that the training direction is firmly imprinted on their memory. Lazy collectors are caught, killed, and replaced by better ones.

Since Kalmus, as far as we can see, did not observe these precautions, and since our experiments showed an unambiguous result (Fig. 62), we must again conclude that the computation of solar movement corresponding to geographic location cannot be completely innate. Of course, each bee will instinctively, on all her flights, observe the position of the sun and its change in angle. But its apparent speed and direction of movement must be learned according to the location. Experiments of another type will confirm these results.

~ Orientation of Bees Raised Without Sun ~

One can let bees hatch in an incubator, and then raise them in the absence of daylight in the cellar by artificial illumination (the day-night rhythm is automatically regulated through a time switch). If it is true that bees must learn locally the calculation of the path of the sun, then such cellar bees should not be able to use the sun compass in their flights during the first days in which they are allowed out of doors. And this is actually the case.

I took bees that had been raised for 4 weeks in artificial light, without sun, out of the cellar into the field at noon, opened the flight entrance, and trained 30 foragers to a feeding table 180 meters to the south. When on the following morning, removed to a strange territory, they were given the opportunity of finding the training direction (south) they were disoriented. The feeding table to the south was *not* more heavily visited than those set up in the north, east, and west (Fig. 63). These bees, reared without sun, thus behave differently from experienced collector bees.

The same bees were then allowed to fly freely for 8 days in the sun, and afterward the same transposition experiment was repeated. This time, after displacement, the collectors flew accurately in the training direction to the south, thereby showing that they had *learned* the sun's course within 8 days.

It would be interesting to know in detail *how* the bees learn to calculate the sun's course. Do they observe the altered position of the sun from time to time throughout the

121

day, and combine this with their exceptional time sense? Or is it sufficient that they become aware of only a part of the sun's course, with its characteristic direction of movement and its speed, in order to calculate from this the other sectors of the arc? The following experiment will explain the process that actually takes place.

A new colony was raised in the cellar in the absence of sunlight, and after 4 weeks brought again into the daylight. These bees were allowed to see only the *afternoon sun each day;* mornings and evenings they were kept in the dark cellar. This was repeated for 35 days. In this way the bees were given the opportunity to commit to memory only the *afternoon course* of the sun. At this point, they were tested to

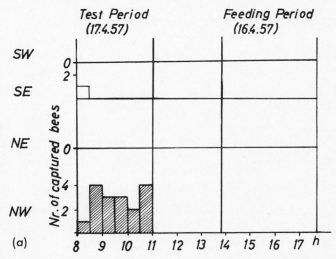

FIG. 62. Two displacement experiments in Brazil, with bees whose ancestors came from North America. The bees were trained to the northwest in the afternoon. On the following morning, after displacement into a strange territory, they again flew to the food table in the training direction. Therefore they had calculated the path of the sun

(*Continued on next page*)

see whether they could find, in the *morning,* a compass point learned by training in the *afternoon.* They were again trained in the afternoon, to a food source in the south, and shifted in the evening to strange territory. In the morning, on the test flights, they were exactly oriented to south. Thus they showed that they could *calculate* the sun's position in the forenoon, extrapolating from their information about *a small part of the sun's course in the afternoon,* and this *when they never before in their lives had seen the morning sun.* The same

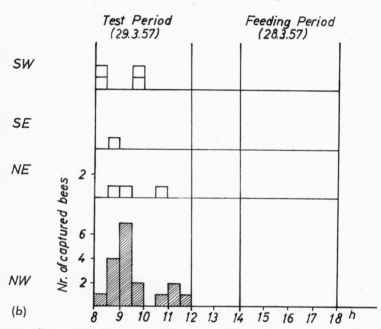

according to their location, and not according to their ancestral land of origin. (As in the experiments of Kalmus, the bees used in experiment (*a*) were the descendants of a queen bee that had been imported from North America a few weeks before. The bees used in experiment (*b*) were descendants of a queen bee that had been imported from North America 4 years before.

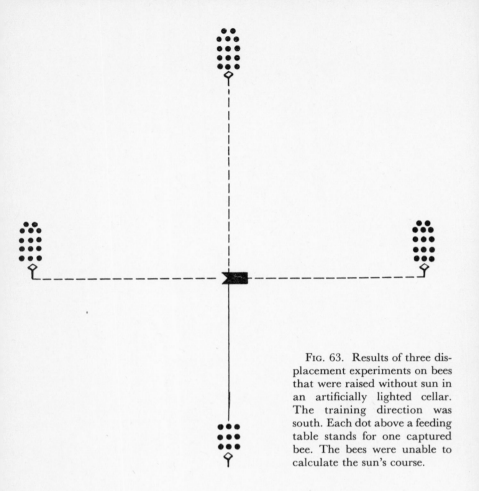

Fig. 63. Results of three displacement experiments on bees that were raised without sun in an artificially lighted cellar. The training direction was south. Each dot above a feeding table stands for one captured bee. The bees were unable to calculate the sun's course.

ability is displayed by the marathon dancers, which dance during the night, extrapolating the position of the sun at a time at which the sun has never been visible to them (see page 95).

In order to analyze the learning process more exactly, I computed the necessary interval of time for the free flight. This was done over a period of eight afternoons. In addition, the number of flights was recorded. A marked collecting

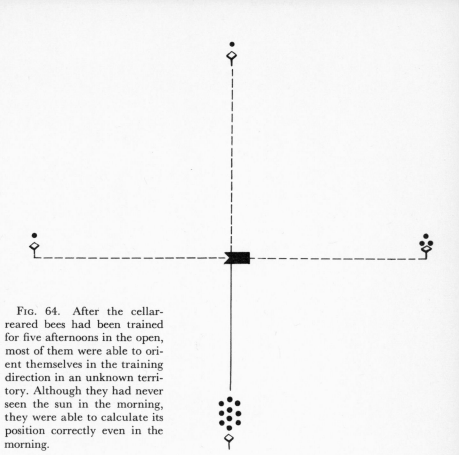

Fig. 64. After the cellar-reared bees had been trained for five afternoons in the open, most of them were able to orient themselves in the training direction in an unknown territory. Although they had never seen the sun in the morning, they were able to calculate its position correctly even in the morning.

swarm was attracted to a feeding table in the south, and all the collecting flights of each bee were recorded. The results showed that, for bees raised without sun, one afternoon outdoors with about 60 collecting flights was *not* sufficient for learning sun orientation. After about five afternoons, with a total of 500 collecting flights, the learning period for sun-compass orientation was almost finished (Fig. 64).

By this means we found one of the first stages of learning in bees raised without sun. Bees that had experienced *three* afternoons of training, with about 300 flights, had learned

125

something, namely, to take into account the *angle* between the sun and the feeding place. The feeding place was located to the south and the afternoon sun was to its right. The next morning the bees, released in strange territory, did not fly to the south, but showed a preference for an *easterly* direction. In other words, they flew true to a solar direction, in such a way that they had the sun again to their right, as on the previous afternoon. This direct "angle-orientation" by means of the solar compass appears to be the first step in the process of learning. After that the bees then learn in addition to calculate the sun's course and its correct azimuth (Lindauer, 1959).

~ The Solar Compass in Competition with Terrestrial Landmarks ~

Now that we had learned the importance of the solar compass for the orientation of bees, we tried to set up landmarks to compete with the sun as reference points for orientation. It has long been known that bees also use landmarks for their orientation—a tree, a path, a forest margin.

Again we made use of the displacement experiment. This time, however, we placed our bee colony on the edge of a wood that ran in a straight line from north to south and bordered on a large, open field. The bees were then trained to a feeding table 180 meters to the south, so that they had the noticeable wood to their right during the flight to the feeding place(Fig. 65). Then we moved the colony overnight to another area, whose chief landmarks were similar to those of the training place. Here the edge of a wood also bordered on an open field, but now the wood ran from east to west instead of from north to south (Fig. 66). The entire landscape was thus turned through an angle of 90°, while the sun remained in its usual course. Would the bees be confused by this striking landmark, or would they be directed by their solar compass and fly out into the open field?

The result was conclusive: the bees were almost unanimously led astray to the west by the edge of the wood. *The*

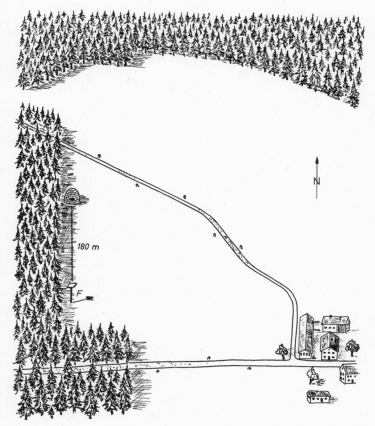

FIG. 65. The bees were offered noticeable terrestrial landmarks during training. In this experiment, they had the edge of a tall wood to their right during their flights to the food table.

127

sun lost out to the terrestrial landmark (von Frisch and Lindauer, 1954).

We repeated the experiment, but this time we set up the hive 60 meters from the edge of the wood and trained the bees as usual to the south. The result was the same. But at a distance of 210 meters, when the wood was to be seen as a narrow shadow-contour only 3–4° above the horizon, the bees no longer observed the edge of the wood as a

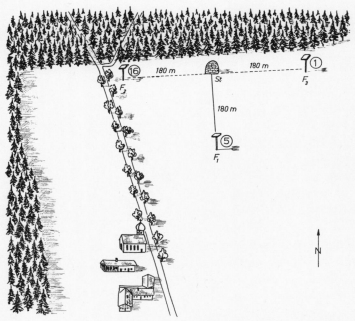

FIG. 66. On the next morning, the southerly-trained bees (Fig. 65) were confronted with a similar terrain, but this time the wood ran east and west instead of north and south. Most bees were lead astray by the terrestrial orientation clues leading west; only a few followed the solar compass. (Numbers at the feeding places indicate numbers of visiting bees captured there.)

guiding line, but they followed the solar compass out into the open field.

We also set up other landmarks in competition with the sun. When we trained the bees on the shore of a lake, which ran in a straight line from east to west, and then on the next morning freed them in another area where the landscape was rotated through 90°, they were again led astray by the terrestrial landmark. All flew to the south, because they had noticed the striking shoreline to the left of their path of flight. The sun also lost out when we trained the bees along a street and repeated the experiment the next morning along another street that lay at a 90° angle to the first.

A characteristic of these dominant landmarks was that they led the bees *in an unbroken line from hive to goal.* In an additional experiment we offered the bees landmarks of another kind. In the training, a large tree stood in the middle of the path of flight between the hive and the feeding place, and it was a particularly striking landmark in the middle of an open meadow. On the next morning, the displaced bees flew out of the hive and saw a similar tree standing in the field—not, however, in a southery direction as on the previous day, but to the east. *This time* the bees did not bother with the beckoning landmark in the distance, but followed the solar compass and flew to the south (Fig. 67).

A rather large group of trees, which lay between the hive and the feeding place, and which on the next morning was correspondingly transposed, was likewise unable to compete with the solar compass (Fig. 68). We hope in the future to obtain a more exact picture of the importance of different landmarks. Perhaps there are some that are an equal match for the solar compass; but to establish this many additional experiments are necessary.

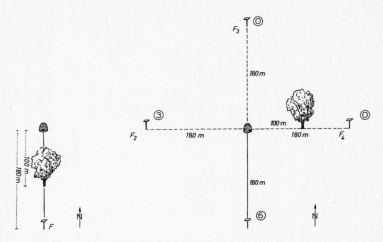

FIG. 67. The bees were *not* led astray by such a striking orientation landmark as a single tree; in this case they faithfully followed their solar compass.

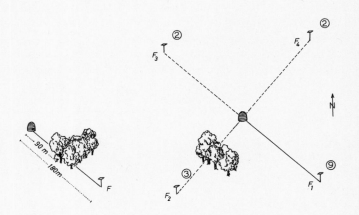

FIG. 68. Again the bees used the sun rather than a group of trees as a guide. (Numbers of bees captured at the various feeding places are shown.)

~ Conclusion ~

When Professor von Frisch reported, in 1946, that bees can inform each other in the dark hive about the position of any point in the surrounding territory, through directed, rhythmic tail-wagging dances, nobody suspected in their first amazement what a wide field for future investigations had been opened up by this discovery.

At first the discovery seemed to concern only comparative animal psychology, since it was a completely new mode of communication, unique in its rich symbolic content. But soon new problems and possibilities appeared in the realm of sensory physiology: it was necessary to investigate the specific sensory faculties that are the basis of this communication system. In the course of this investigation, new high levels of accomplishment in insect sensory organs were discovered, which nobody would have anticipated before.

Finally, the question of the phylogenetic development led us to undertake studies in "comparative linguistics" among the taxonomic relatives of *Apis mellifera*. And in carrying out these studies, we have already found several modifications and some primitive rudiments of the honeybees' dance, as well as new forms of communication that can be considered independent sidelines of development, branching from the common primitive elements of the bee's dance. With such investigations, it has been shown that phylogenetic research is possible even in the field of such highly developed behavioral characteristics—which do not leave paleontological traces, such as fossils, as proof of their part in phylogenetic history.

REFERENCES

Baltzer, F. "Einige Beobachtungen über Sicheltänze bei Bienenvölkern verschiedener Herkunft," *Arch. Julius Klaus-Stift.* 27, 197–206 (1952).

Baumgärtner, H. "Der Formensinn und die Sehschärfe der Bienen," *Z. vergleich Physiol.* 7, 56–143 (1929).

Baunacke, W. "Statische Sinnesorgane bei den Nepiden," *Zool. Jahrb., Abt. Anat.* 34, 179–342 (1912).

Beling, I., "Über das Zeitgedächtnis der Bienen," *Z. vergleich. Physiol.* 9 259–338 (1929).

Birukow, G., "Photo-Geomenotaxis bei *Geotrupes silvaticus* Panz.," *Naturwissenschaften* 40, 61–62 (1953).

—— "Photo-Geomenotaxis bei *Geotrupes silvaticus* Panz. und ihre zentralnervöse Koordination," *Z. vergleich. Physiol.* 36, 176–211 (1954).

Bisetzky, A. R., "Die Tänze der Bienen nach einem Fussweg zum Futterplatz," *Z. vergleich, Physiol.* 40, 264–288, (1957).

Boch, R., "Rassenmässige Unterschiede in den Tänzen der Honigbiene (*Apis mellifica* L.)," *Z. vergleich. Physiol.* 39, 289–320 (1957).

Brian, M. V., "Food collection by a Scottish ant community," *J. animal Ecol.* 24, 336–351 (1955).

Carthy, J. D., "The orientation of two allied species of British ants. II: Odour trail laying and following in *Acanthomyops* (*Lasius*) *fuliginosus*," *Behaviour 3*, 304–318 (1951).

Del Portillo, J., "Beziehungen zwischen den Öffnungswinkeln der Ommatidien, Krümmung und Gestalt der Insektenaugen und ihrer funktionellen Aufgabe," *Z. vergleich. Physiol. 23*, 100–145 (1936).

Dethier, V. G., "Communication by insects: physiology of dancing," *Science 125*, 331–336 (1957).

Frisch, K. von, "Die Tänze der Bienen," *Österr. zool. Z. 1*, 1–48 (1946).

——— "Gelöste und ungelöste Rätsel der Bienensprache," *Naturwissenschaften 35*, 12–23; 38–43 (1948).

——— "Die Polarisation des Himmelslichtes als orientierender Faktor bei den Tänzen der Bienen," *Experientia 5*, 142–148 (1949).

——— "Die Sonne als Kompass im Leben der Bienen," *Experientia 6*, 210–221 (1950).

——— *Bees: their Vision, Chemical Senses and Language* (Cornell University Press, Ithaca, N. Y., 1950).

——— "Orientierungsvermögen und Sprache der Bienen," *Naturwissenschaften 38*, 105–112 (1951).

——— "Die Fähigkeit der Bienen, die Sonne durch die Wolken wahrzunehmen," *Sitzber. bayer. Akad. Wiss.*, No. 14, 197 (1953).

——— "Sprechende Tänze im Bienenvolk," Festrede in der Bayer. Akad. Wiss. (1954).

Frisch, K. von, H. Heran, and M. Lindauer, "Gibt es in der 'Sprache' der Bienen eine Weisung nach oben und unten?" *Z. vergleich, Physiol. 35*, 219–245 (1953).

Frisch, K. von, and M. Lindauer, "Himmel und Erde in Konkurrenz bei der Orientierung der Bienen," *Naturwissenschaften 41*, 245–253 (1954).

——— "Über die Fluggeschwindigkeit der Bienen und über ihre Richtungsweisung bei Seitenwind," *Naturwissenschaften 42*, 377–385 (1955).

Frisch, K. von, M. Lindauer, and F. Schmeidler, "Wie erkennt die Biene den Sonnenstand bei geschlossener Wolkendecke?" *Naturw. Rundschau 10*, 1–7 (1960).

Goetsch, W., *Vergleichende Biologie der Insektenstaaten* (Leipzig, 1953).

Haas, A., "Neue Beobachtungen zum Problem der Flugbahnen bei Hummelmännchen," *Z. Naturforsch. 1*, 596–600 (1946).

—— "Gesetzmässiges Flugverhalten der Männchen von *Psithyrus silvestris* und einiger solitärer Apiden," *Z. vergleich. Physiol. 31*, 281–307 (1949).

—— "Die Mandibeldrüse als Duftorgan bei einigen Hymenopteren," *Naturwissenschaften 39*, 484 (1952).

Hein, G., "Über richtungsweisende Bienentänze bei Futterplätzen in Stocknähe," *Experientia 6*, 142–144 (1950).

Heran, H., "Ein Beitrag zur Frage nach der Wahrnehmungsgrundlage der Entfernungsweisung der Bienen (*Apis mellifica* L.)," *Z. vergleich, Physiol. 38*, 168–218 (1956).

Heran, H., and L. Wanke, "Beobachtungen über die Entfernungsmeldungen der Sammelbienen," *Z. vergleich. Physiol. 34*, 383–393 (1952).

Holt, S. J., "On the foraging activity of the wood ant," *J. animal Ecol. 24*, 1–33 (1951).

Jacobs-Jessen, U. F., "Zur Orientierung der Hummeln und einiger anderer Hymenopteren," *Z. vergleich. Physiol. 41*, 597–641 (1959).

Jander, R., "Die optische Richtungsorientierung der roten Waldameise (*Formica rufa* L.)," *Z. vergleich. Physiol. 40*, 162–238 (1957).

Kalmus, H., "Sun navigation by animals," *Nature 174*, 657–659 (1954).

—— "Sun navigation of *Apis mellifica* L. in the southern hemisphere," *J. Exptl. Biol. 33*, 554–565 (1956).

Lindauer, M., "Ein Beitrag zur Frage der Arbeitsteilung im Bienenstaat," *Z. vergleich. Physiol. 34*, 299–345 (1952).

—— "Bienentänze in der Schwarmtraube," *Naturwissenschaften 38*, 509–513 (1951); *40*, 379–385 (1953).

—— "Temperaturregulierung und Wasserhaushalt im Bienenstaat," *Z. vergleich. Physiol. 36*, 391–432 (1954).

—— "Schwarmbienen auf Wohnungssuche," *Z. vergleich. Physiol. 37*, 263–324 (1955).

—— "Über die Verständigung bei indischen Bienen," *Z. vergleich. Physiol. 38*, 521–557 (1956).

—— "Sonnenorientierung der Bienen unter der Äquatorsonne und zur Nachtzeit," *Naturwissenschaften 44*, 1–6 (1957).

—— "Die gegenseitige Verständigung bei den stachellosen Bienen," *Z. vergleich Physiol. 41*, 405–434 (1958).

—— "Angeborene und erlernte Komponenten in der Sonnenorientierung der Bienen. Bemerkungen und Versuche zu einer Mitteilung von Kalmus," *Z. vergleich. Physiol. 42*, 43–62 (1959).

Lindauer, M., and W. E. Kerr, "Die gegenseitige Verständigung bei den stachellosen Bienen," *Z. vergleich Physiol. 41*, 405–434 (1958).

Lindauer, M., and J. O. Nedel, "Ein Schweresinnesorgan der Honigbiene," *Z. vergleich. Physiol. 42*, 334–364 (1959).

Lüscher, M., "Zur Frage der Übertragung sozialer Wirkstoffe bei Termiten," *Naturwissenschaften 42*, 186 (1955).

—— "Experimentelle Erzeugung von Soldaten bei der Termite *Kalotermes flavicollis* (Fabr.)," *Naturwissenschaften 45*, 69–70 (1958).

McGregor, E. G., "Odour as a basis for orientated movement in ants," *Behaviour 1*, 267–296 (1948).

Michener, C. D., "Distinctive type of primitive social behavior among bees," *Science 127*, 1046–1047 (1958).

Mittelstaedt, H., "Physiologie des Gleichgewichtssinnes bei fliegenden Libellen," *Z. vergleich. Physiol. 32*, 422–463 (1950).

Park, O. W., "The storing and ripening of honey by honeybees," *J. Econ. Entomol. 18*, 405–410 (1925).

Plateaux, C., née Quénu, "Un nouveau type de société d'insectes: *Halictus marginatus* Brullé," *Thèses présentées à la faculté des sciences de l'université de Paris* (A), No. 3357, 327–439 (1960).

REFERENCES

Rabe, W., "Beiträge zum Orientierungsproblem der Wasser-wanzen," *Z. vergleich. Physiol. 35,* 300–325 (1953).

Renner, M., "Neue Versuche über den Zeitsinn der Honig-biene," *Z. vergleich. Physiol. 40,* 85–118 (1957).

Rösch, G. A., Untersuchungen über die Arbeitsteilung im Bienenstaat," *Z. vergleich. Physiol. 2,* 571–631 (1925); *12,* 1–71 (1930).

—— "Über die Bautätigkeit im Bienenvolk und das Alter der Baubienen," *Z. vergleich. Physiol. 6,* 265–298 (1927).

Steche, W., "Gibt es 'Dialekte' der Bienensprache?" disserta-tion, Faculty of Science, University of Munich (1954).

Sudd, J. H., "Communication and recruitment in pharaos ant," *Brit. J. animal Behav. 5,* 104–109 (1957).

—— "The foraging method of pharaos ant *Monomorium pha-raonis,*" *Animal Behaviour 8,* 67–75 (1959).

Tschumi, P., "Über den Werbetanz der Bienen bei nahen Trachtquellen," *Schweiz. Bienenztg. 73,* 129–134 (1950).

Uchida, T., and M. Kuwabara, "The homing instinct of the honeybee, *Apis mellifica,*" *J. Fac. Sci. Hokkaido Univ.* (6), *10* (1951).

Vowles, D. M., "Orientation and route finding in the Hymen-optera," dissertation, Oxford University, Bodleian Library, 1951.

—— "The orientation of ants. I. The substitution of stimuli," *J. Exptl. Biol. 31,* 341–355 (1954); "II. Orientation to light, gravity and polarized light," *J. Exptl. Biol. 31,* 356–375 (1954).

Weber, H., *Lehrbuch der Entomologie* (Jena, 1933).

Wilson, E. O., "Feeding behavior in the ant *Rhopalotrix biroi szabo,*" *Psyche 63,* 21 (1956).

—— "Source and possible nature of the odor trail of fire ants," *Science 129,* 643–644 (1959).

Wilson, E. O., and T. Eisner, "Quantitative studies of liquid food transmission in ants," *Insectes sociaux 2,* 157–166 (1957).

Wolf, E., "Über das Heimkehrvermögen der Bienen," *Z. ver-gleich. Physiol. 3,* 615–691 (1926); *6,* 221–254 (1927).

Index